AQA History B
Historical Enquiry

GCSE

Alan Mendum
David Ferriby
Tony Hewitt
Jim McCabe

Nelson Thornes

Published in 2009 by:
Nelson Thornes Ltd
Delta Place
27 Bath Road
CHELTENHAM
GL53 7TH
United Kingdom

09 10 11 12 13 / 10 9 8 7 6 5 4 3 2 1

A catalogue record for this book is available from the British Library

978 1 4085 0322 5

Illustrations by David Russell Illustration

Page make-up by Fakenham Photosetting Ltd

Printed in Croatia by Zrinski

Contents

Contents

Nelson Thornes has worked in partnership with AQA to ensure this book and the accompanying online resources offer you the best support for your GCSE course.

All resources have been approved by senior AQA examiners so you can feel assured that they closely match the specification for this subject and provide you with everything you need to prepare successfully for your Historical Enquiry.

These print and online resources together **unlock blended learning**; this means that the links between the activities in the book and the activities online blend together to maximise your understanding of a topic and help you achieve your potential.

These online resources are available on **kerboodle!** which can be accessed via the internet at **www.kerboodle.com/live**, anytime, anywhere. If your school or college subscribes to **kerboodle!** you will be provided with your own personal login details. Once logged in, access your course and locate the required activity.

For more information and help on how to use **kerboodle!** visit **www.kerboodle.com**

How to use this book

Objectives

Look for the list of **Learning Objectives** based on the requirements of this course so you can ensure you are covering everything you need to know for the Historical Enquiry.

AQA Examiner's tip

Don't forget to read the **AQA Examiner's Tips** throughout the book as well as practise answering **Controlled Assessment style Questions**.

Visit **www.nelsonthornes.com/aqagcse** for more information.

AQA Controlled Assessment style questions are reproduced by permission of the Assessment and Qualifications Alliance.

Introduction to the Historical Enquiry

What does the specification say about the Historical Enquiry?

- It consists of 25 per cent of the total marks for History B.
- It requires you to find suitable sources to answer the questions set.
- There are two questions to be answered for your historical enquiry. You will be told the questions by your teacher before you start your research. One question asks you to test the utility (usefulness) of a set of five sources selected by you. The second question asks you to test an interpretation of the past using at least eight sources selected by you.
- You are advised to write about 800 words to answer the first question and 1,200 words to answer the second question.
- Your answers must be produced in **controlled conditions**.

Going about the Historical Enquiry

If you were to consider how an historian finds out about the past, you would probably note the importance of finding *evidence* to tell us about past events. Sometimes that evidence is in the form of **artefacts**. Sometimes the evidence is found looking at buildings or even in the land itself (historical geography). Archive films or newsreels can be used as evidence of the past. For more recent events you might be able to interview someone who has witnessed them (oral evidence). However, the most common types of evidence are found in documents. As it is likely that the sources that you will research in the Historical Enquiry will be very largely documentary in form, the different kinds of documentary evidence are looked at in detail later in this chapter.

Objectives

In this chapter you will learn about:

the requirements of the Historical Enquiry in the specification

how sources should be researched in the Historical Enquiry

the different types of sources that can be used in the Historical Enquiry

the mark schemes for the questions set in the Historical Enquiry.

Key terms

Controlled conditions: under examination conditions.

Artefacts: objects from the past that have been found or kept.

A Artefacts from World War 2

Things to look for in the use of sources

The evidence you have found in the sources must be tested so that you can make the correct use of them. You should ask yourself two questions about a source:

- Is it **reliable** (or accurate)? Can you accept the information that it provides as being true? If not, why not?
- Is it **useful** (utility)? Can you use the information in the source? If not, why not?

The two questions often overlap in reaching a conclusion on the source, but they do not always do so. To take an obvious example: a statement by Hitler on the Jews would not be reliable, but it can be useful because it tells you what Hitler's views on the Jews were.

So how you use a source, and whether it is reliable or useful, will depend on the question that you are asked.

Provenance

The key to understanding a source is to consider its *provenance*:

- **when** was it produced – at the time (*primary* evidence) or later (*secondary* evidence)?
- **who** produced it?
- **why** was it produced?

You can see that by considering these questions you will be able to decide whether and/or how far a source is reliable, useful or accurate. This process is called:

- **source evaluation** (where you examine a source for its reliability or utility)
- **source analysis** (where you examine what the source is saying and what it means – this is much more than *describing* it).

These are phrases that you can see throughout the mark schemes.

Activity

1   Look at any source in this book.
   a   What is the provenance of the source?
   b   From that decide whether the source is reliable, useful and/or accurate.
   c   Take turns to discuss your views with another person.

kerboodle!

Types of sources

There are a number of different types of sources that you are likely to come across in your research. Some will be **primary sources** (first hand); others will be **secondary sources** (second hand). Each has its advantages and its limitations.

Written primary source

This is likely to be one of the most common types of source that you will see. To decide how reliable or useful it is, you must look at the provenance – in particular why it was written and who wrote it.

> ❝ *This morning every one of the 1700 coal mines in Britain will pass out of the hands of private owners and become the property of the people. There will be a simple ceremony in London. At dawn trumpets will echo through the valleys of South Wales with bands playing and children singing.* ❞
>
> From Daily Herald, *1 January 1947*

B *The nationalisation of the coal industry, 1947*

The newspaper account gives a factual account of the event so it can be accepted as accurate and reliable. It is also useful in describing the attitude of the people of South Wales to the nationalisation of the coal industry.

Comment

> ❝ *The Suffragettes marched on the House of Commons yesterday, and the scenes witnessed exceeded in violence anything that these militant women had previously been guilty of. It was an unending picture of shameful recklessness. Never before have otherwise sensible women gone so far in forgetting their womanhood. The police kept their tempers admirably even though some were assaulted by angry women. There were 120 arrests.* ❞
>
> From Daily Sketch, *19 November 1910*

C *An account of the Suffragette demonstration to Parliament*

There are parts of this newspaper report that are accurate – the demonstration did take place; there were 120 arrests. However, if you look at the description of the event and the language used, you can see the bias against the Suffragettes. So you may doubt that this is a *reliable* account of the event.

Comment

Key terms

Primary source: produced *at the time* of an event. A newspaper is an obvious example but it could be a diary, a cartoon, a photograph. Primary sources are usually intended for the audience at the time of the event – this makes them useful to historians.

Secondary source: produced *after* the event. A book written by an historian is an obvious example. This will usually be more balanced and unbiased than a primary source because it has the benefit of hindsight.

Written secondary source

This kind of source will often be written by an historian. Therefore you can generally accept that it will be accurate and reliable. Whether it is useful will depend on how it links to the question you are answering. For example, if you are researching the fighting on the Western Front in the First World War, a book on the Battle of the Marne, 1914, will have only a limited utility. However, do not assume that every secondary source is reliable.

> 66 *As to whether it was wise or foolish for General Haig to give battle on the Somme, there can be only one opinion. To have refused to fight then and there would have meant the abandonment of the French in their defence of the fortress of Verdun. This would have meant the breakdown of all co-operation with the French.* 99
>
> From Haig, the official biography written by the historian Duff Cooper at the request of Haig's family, published 1936

D *An historian's comment on the Battle of the Somme*

> **Comment**
>
> A reading of this source by an historian might suggest that it is reliable. However, a look at the provenance might make you think again. Can a book written at the request of the Haig family be completely unbiased and reliable?

A *novel* may also be classed as a secondary source. You must look carefully at who the author is (e.g. has the author lived through the period in which the book is written?) and why the book has been produced. If it has been produced for entertainment or profit would this affect its reliability and usefulness?

> 66 *Miss Evans looked down at their feet. 'Better change into your slippers before I take you to your bedroom.' 'We haven't any,' Carrie said. She meant to explain that that there hadn't been room in their cases for slippers, but before she could speak Miss Evans turned bright red and said 'Oh, I'm sorry, why should you have slippers? Never mind just keep to the middle of the stair carpet where it's covered with a cloth.' Her brother Nick whispered, 'She thinks we're poor children, too poor to have slippers,' and they giggled.* 99
>
> From Carrie's War, a novel by Nina Bawden, 1973

E *An extract from a novel about evacuees*

> **Comment**
>
> The source is useful as it tells us about how people who took in evacuees could react to them. However, it is from a novel – a piece of fiction – written almost 40 years after the event and written for children – this could make it unreliable.

Visual sources

There are a variety of **visual sources** that you are likely to find in your research. They can be very effective in bringing the past to life – but they can have as many limitations as advantages. Again a consideration of the provenance will help you to make the correct judgement on the sources. The most common kinds of visual sources are the following:

Photographs

The old advice that 'the camera never lies' is not true. A photograph can easily be staged. So you must look at *why* the photograph was taken – what was the purpose? A photograph is also a 'snapshot' of one time in one place. It may not represent what is happening elsewhere.

Key terms

Visual source: includes photographs, paintings, posters, cartoons. These are usually primary sources produced at the time of the event. A film is a visual source that can be primary or secondary, depending on when it is made.

 *The evacuation of children in the Second World War*

Comment

This source can be very useful as it shows part of the process of evacuation. However, its reliability can be questioned. It is one of a number of photographs issued by the government to make evacuation look appealing and to encourage parents to allow their children to be evacuated.

Posters

Posters are generally issued for two reasons: to give information; or to persuade you to do something – to buy a particular product, or to vote for a particular party. In the second case the poster is a piece of propaganda. Governments often use posters as propaganda to get a message across – particularly in wartime to try to help the war effort. This means that such posters may not be reliable. However, they can be useful because they tell you what the government *thought* was important at that time to help in winning the war.

H *A government poster from the First World War, issued in 1916*

> This is certainly useful in telling you how important the government thought the role of women was in the First World War. In this case, can you identify what the government was trying to persuade women to do?
>
> *Comment*

Paintings

A painting can be very subjective – it is usually a personal view. Again look for the purpose of the painting – why has the artist painted it? You are likely to come across 'official artists', especially during the two World Wars. These were artists commissioned (paid) by the government to make paintings of important events. This could affect their reliability because, like posters, the government may be trying to use them for propaganda.

1 Retreat from Dunkirk, 1940, *painted by Charles Cundall, a British government war artist*

This cannot have been painted *as the actual evacuation was taking place* so it is an artist's impression, *painted after the event,* of what happened at Dunkirk. Also the artist was commissioned by the government to paint it so you should ask what message the government was trying to give about Dunkirk. However, it does contain a lot of detail. Your knowledge of the event could test its accuracy.

Comment

Cartoons

A cartoon is a visual comment on an event usually published at the time of the event. It is often satirical but not necessarily funny. It is likely to be biased because it will exaggerate an event. This may affect its accuracy and reliability. However, it can be useful because it may tell you what was thought about an event at the time it was happening. As always, you should look very carefully at the provenance of the cartoon. Try to work out what the cartoonist is making fun of – this will tell you which side the cartoonist is on.

Major-General (addressing the men before practising an attack behind the lines). "I WANT YOU TO UNDERSTAND THAT THERE IS A DIFFERENCE BETWEEN A REHEARSAL AND THE REAL THING. THERE ARE THREE ESSENTIAL DIFFERENCES: FIRST, THE ABSENCE OF THE ENEMY. NOW *(turning to the Regimental Sergeant-Major)* WHAT IS THE SECOND DIFFERENCE?"
Sergeant-Major. "THE ABSENCE OF THE GENERAL, SIR."

J *A comment on officers in the First World War, published in the British magazine* Punch *in February 1917*

> The cartoon is not accurate – the event never happened. It is not reliable as it is clearly making fun of officers. However, it might be useful in presenting a popular view of officers in the First World War – at the front and at home.
>
> **Comment**

Films

This is a broad area. Archive film (film shot at the time of an event) can be useful – but it does depend on its provenance. Old newsreels are likely to be the most useful source. Feature films, made after the event, can be useful in giving you an impression of an event. However, while many films try to achieve historical accuracy, the main aim of a film is to develop the story line and the characters in it in an entertaining way.

Diagrams with data

As these contain lists of figures, they are likely to be accurate, reliable and useful. However, you have to interpret the data so it is important not to read too much into them and come to conclusions that the data does not really support. Above all you need to link the data to the question you are researching.

K *A family budget from the 1930s: Alfred Smith lived on unemployment benefit*

	Old Money	New Money
Rent	14s 6d	73p
Clothes	6s 0d	30p
Insurance	1s 8d	7p
Coal	3s 0d	15p
Coke	1s 0d	5p
Lighting	3s 0d	15p
Bread	6s 0d	30p
Other food	16s 0d	80p
TOTAL	£2 11s 2d	£2.55

> **Comment**
>
> You can accept the information in the source as accurate. However, it only represents one person's income and expenditure – so it may not be typical of anyone else's spending. Nor does it tell you if Alfred Smith had any other income. Equally, it might be useful as an example of the kinds of problems faced by people on unemployment benefit in the 1930s.

Maps

These are diagrams that give a visual impression of an event. They are also likely to have additional information that will be accurate. However, as with data, maps should be used with care. They will only contain the information that the map's author wants to include – so there may be important 'gaps' in terms of the question you are researching.

Oral evidence

You may be fortunate enough to know somebody who has lived through the event you are researching – perhaps somebody who has been evacuated or who has fought in the Second World War or lived through the Depression of the 1930s. This is a useful source of evidence and you should take the opportunity to find out about the past from someone with a direct knowledge of it. However, there can be problems with **oral sources**. The person's memory may be faulty or selective. There may be a tendency to exaggerate. If possible you should use other information to test the accuracy of oral evidence.

Oral evidence is increasingly collected in books and on websites; it has been written down and edited. This can help bridge the gap between now and an event that occurred some time ago (like the First World War) from which few people are still alive. It allows you to use oral evidence in your research. However, the same problems can arise as with a 'live' interview.

Key terms

Oral source: spoken evidence of an event. It could be a one-to-one interview with a person who has lived through an event, or a recording (on tape or in writing) of a person speaking about an event.

Activity

2 a Turn to the chapter that covers the topic you are studying for your historical enquiry. Copy out Table **L** below, adding more rows as needed.

   b Then look at all the sources in the chapter and complete the appropriate boxes.

   c Compare your answers with others in your group.

L

Source	Written secondary	Written primary	Visual type	Reliable	Useful	Accurate
e.g. A			cartoon	x	yes	x

Understanding the mark schemes

The two questions that you will be given test different skills in your historical enquiry. Your teacher will discuss the mark schemes in greater detail with you. This section will explain the mark schemes to you in simple terms to guide you on how to answer the two questions. Each mark scheme has four levels with a range of marks in each level. The levels represent different levels of quality in your answers. You should be aiming for the higher levels.

Question 1: Testing the utility of sources

The question is worth 15 marks. You should aim to write about 800 words in your answer.

> **'Select five sources. Explain how useful these sources have been in informing you in your historical enquiry.'**

Level 1

is an answer that only describes the sources and simply accepts that they are useful without trying to explain why. You can see that such an answer will not really tackle the question set.

Level 2

is an answer that looks in greater depth at the sources and moves beyond only describing them by making some comments on the content – an attempt at *source analysis*. The answer also makes simple, general comments on the usefulness of the sources: e.g. 'this source is a photograph so it cannot be completely reliable because it could have been posed or set up'.

Level 3

is a more detailed (developed) answer than Level 2. It looks at the meaning of the sources in some depth by explaining what the sources are saying (*source analysis*). It also provides some *knowledge* to support or reject the content of the sources. By doing these two things you will be able to consider the usefulness and the limitations of the sources. A Level 3 answer may also go further than Level 2 in *evaluating* the sources by looking at the provenance of each of them.

Level 4

builds on Level 3 and is an answer that consistently demonstrates the three skills over all five sources.

- *source evaluation* by looking at provenance, reliability and limitations of the five sources in deciding their usefulness
- *source analysis* in explaining the meaning of the sources to judge their usefulness
- good use of supporting *knowledge* to test the usefulness of the sources.

A Level 4 answer should also make a *judgement* on how useful the five sources have been in your historical enquiry.

Key terms

Mark scheme: a scheme detailing how credit is to be awarded in relation to a particular unit, component or task. A mark scheme normally characterises acceptable answers or levels of response to questions/tasks or parts of questions/tasks and identifies the amount of credit each attracts.

AQA *Examiner's tip*

In selecting the five sources make sure that you get a good *balance* of sources so that you can answer the question in sufficient depth to reach Level 3 or 4. A good balance means two things:

- the use of different types of sources
- the selection of some sources that you think are useful and some that are not so useful.

Your answer can then explain more fully why some sources are useful and others less so.

Try to avoid general comments on the sources. Make your comments relate to the particular sources you have chosen.

Question 2: Testing an interpretation

The question is worth 25 marks. You should aim to write about 1,200 words in your answer.

> **You should select at least eight sources. The question will then ask you how far the sources support an interpretation that you will be given.**

Level 1

is an answer that accepts the content of the sources and describes them. As in Question 1, this kind of answer will not tackle the question that you have been set.

Level 2

is an answer that covers a number of points in a simple way:

- examining what the sources are saying (*source analysis*) to show that there is enough **or** not enough evidence to agree with the interpretation stated in the question
- using some *knowledge* to support or reject the source content
- involving some source *evaluation* but with only simple, general comments.

Level 3

is an answer of greater depth than Level 2 – one which shows a better understanding of the issues involved in the interpretation. The same three points covered in Level 2 are still present but the answer is more developed:

- examining the meaning of the content of the sources (*source analysis*) in a depth to show that there is evidence to agree **and** disagree with the interpretation
- using *knowledge* to support and reject the content of the sources
- *evaluating* the sources by looking at the provenance of each of them.

A Level 3 answer should also try to explain the reasons why some sources support the interpretation and others do not.

Level 4

further builds on the three skills covered in Levels 2 and 3. It expects all three skills to be present in an answer in a more detailed way. In particular:

- the *evaluation* of the sources should be at a greater depth. Provenance, purpose, reliability, limitations should all be considered.
- the answer should also make a *balanced judgement*. This means that you may support or disagree with the interpretation **so long as** you examine both points of view. You may also partly agree and partly disagree with the interpretation – but again explain why you have come to this conclusion.

AQA **Examiner's tip**

- As for Question 1 you should select a good balance of sources so that you can discuss the interpretation in depth. Again look for a balance of different types of sources. It is also important to get a balance of sources that can agree and disagree with the interpretation – only by doing this will you be able to achieve the balanced answer required for Level 3 and 4.
- It does not matter what conclusion you reach about the interpretation so long as the sources used in the enquiry can support your conclusion.
- Evaluate and analyse each source for what it says, **not** for the type of source it is. In this way you will avoid simple, general answers.

⚭links

Now that you have read this introduction you might want to test your understanding of the mark schemes by looking at the sample answers and comments provided in Chapter 5.

1 The British people in war

1.1 Britain in the First World War, 1914–18

Attitudes to war

When war was declared in August 1914 there was much enthusiasm. Germany had invaded Belgium and Britain was going to the defence of her ally. Nobody knew, of course, that the war was going to involve the death of millions and last over four years. It was expected that the war would be short; the soldiers would be home by Christmas.

So at the beginning of August 1914 – a bank holiday weekend – there was a lot of excitement. Many people were on holiday. The weather was hot; the beaches were crowded; people appeared to be enjoying themselves. Yet at the same time the British army, the British Expeditionary Force (BEF), was on the move towards the ports.

Most British people were patriotic; they supported their country and assumed that Britain was in the right and that Germany was in the wrong. The powerful British Empire would also be able to provide troops, and, with the great British navy patrolling the seas, British victory was thought to be inevitable.

Objectives

In this chapter you will learn about:

how the First and Second World Wars changed the way of life of the people of Britain

how far and why the experience of British people at war in the First World War differed from their experience in the Second World War

developing skills of source evaluation to test the reliability, utility and accuracy of evidence

evaluating a number of sources to test an interpretation.

A Crowds cheering at the declaration of war in Trafalgar Square, London, August 1914

B *Patriotic women gather outside a house persuading men to join and serve for England, 1914*

Task

1 Do Sources **A** and **B** give the same view of British attitudes to war when it started in August 1914? Explain your answer.

The Defence of the Realm Act

The British government passed the Defence of the Realm Act (DORA) in the first month of the war. It gave the government much more power over people's lives. Railways and coal mines were taken over by the government. People could be told where to work. Pub opening hours were cut; beer was watered down. Through DORA and in other ways, the war quickly affected all British civilians – not just the armed forces. Although Britain was not in real danger of invasion, everyone was involved in the fighting.

As war continued during the next four years, people became less enthusiastic. Many became openly hostile, especially as the casualty figures rose alarmingly and many families were affected by the death of or injury to at least one family member.

Some men refused to fight and kill. These men were called conscientious objectors. Often the general public was not very sympathetic towards them. They were assumed to be slackers or cowards. In fact, it took considerable bravery for these men (16,000 of them) to stand up for what they believed in, considering the abuse that was often hurled at them by family and friends. Many of these COs took on war jobs, such as driving ambulances or acting as nurses. However, about 1,500 refused to have anything to do with the war, and they were imprisoned. Some died in prison.

Did you know ??????

Under DORA the British public were not allowed to fly a kite or light a bonfire because these could attract Zeppelins, and they were not allowed to waste food by feeding bread to wild animals.

Did you know ??????

Conscientious objectors were often known as 'conchies' or 'COs'.

Recruitment and conscription

At the outbreak of war the British army was small. Lord Kitchener, the War Minister, asked for volunteers. One million volunteered by the end of 1914. Men went to fight in what became known as 'Pals Battalions'. These were made up of men from the same town or group of villages; they trained together and fought together. The effect, however, was that in a battle huge numbers of friends from one small area could all be killed within days – leaving a community in Britain to mourn.

Men were under considerable pressure to volunteer. In cities such as London, women went round giving out white feathers to able-bodied young men who were not in uniform. Patriotism was whipped up through marches, public meetings, and songs sung in music-hall entertainments. Government posters were also used.

Did you know ??????
White feathers were traditionally a symbol of cowardice.

C *A British army recruitment poster of 1914. It is Lord Kitchener's finger that is pointing*

D *A government poster of 1914*

F A call for more recruits – a government poster in the first years of the war

> 66 *Oh we don't want to lose you,*
> *But we think you ought to go,*
> *For your King and your country*
> *Both need you so.*
>
> *We shall want you and miss you,*
> *But with all our might and main,*
> *We shall cheer you, thank you, kiss you,*
> *When you come back again.* 99
>
> *By Paul Rubens, a popular Edwardian songwriter*

E A recruitment song of 1914

Although by 1916 the figure had risen to over 2 million, as the war continued the number of volunteers got fewer and fewer. At the same time, thousands of men were being killed or badly injured fighting. Therefore, the government was forced to introduce conscription – that is, men had to join. The Military Service Act was passed in January 1916, and all single men aged between 18 and 41 could be called up. This was extended in May 1916 to married men. In practice, men in some occupations were excluded, such as miners and engine drivers, as their work was essential in Britain.

Did you know ? ? ? ? ?

Before the Military Service Act was extended to include married men, it was nicknamed the 'Bachelor's Bill'.

Task

2   How useful are Sources **C**, **D**, **E** and **F** for learning about why men joined the British army? Use the sources and your own knowledge to explain your answer.

Enemy attacks on Britain

This was the first war where civilians were directly involved. In December 1914 people in Hartlepool, Scarborough and Whitby on the north-east coast of England suffered from shelling by German ships. There were over 500 civilian casualties. The raids were a shock, but they did help to unite the people of Britain against the Germans.

Civilians were also affected by the German **U-boat** campaign. The Germans used their submarines in an effort to starve Britain out of the war.

Enemy attacks also came from the air. The Germans had developed Zeppelin airships. The attacks started in 1915 and continued into 1916. Zeppelins could travel at 85 miles per hour and carry up to 2 tons of bombs. Some east coast cities and towns suffered bomb damage. The first raid was on Great Yarmouth and King's Lynn in Norfolk in January 1915 and then Hull in June 1915. The inland port of Goole (up the river Humber) also suffered a raid that missed the target of the docks but destroyed several houses in the town and killed 27 people.

The main target, of course, was London. The first Zeppelin raid on London was at midnight on 31 May 1915, killing seven people and doing £18,000 worth of damage. Nearer the end of the war the air threat came from German planes which killed over 1,000 people, as well as damaging many houses and businesses. The German Gotha planes were generally more successful at night when there was a moon. Pilots used the river Thames as a guide to finding targets in London. Because of these attacks many Londoners hid overnight in underground railway stations – a sight more commonly thought of in connection with the Second World War and the Blitz.

Home defence

The German attacks on Britain, especially those from the air, showed that civilians were greatly at risk, especially those living near the east coast. The government had to act to defend its citizens.

The British fleet was used to guard the east coast from further attacks by sea. Some British ships were used to blockade German ports so that German ships were trapped there. In 1917 the British navy started using the convoy system, with merchant ships sailing in groups with British navy protection. This helped to deal with the threat to food supplies and ensured that British people would not starve.

Defences were developed against air attacks. Barrage balloons were used against Zeppelins. Large guns were positioned on the ground so that a Zeppelin, when spotted, could be fired at. If it was hit, it would burst into flames because it was filled with hydrogen. Towards the end of the war other measures were introduced that foreshadowed what would be done in the Second World War, such as blackout curtains to make it more difficult for German bombers to see their targets.

Key terms

U-boat: German: *U-Boot*, or (in full) *Unterseeboot*. English: U-boat or submarine.

⃟links

For details on food shortages, see page 23 (First World War) and page 33 (Second World War).

Did you know ??????

Count von Zeppelin flew his first airship in 1900. They were lighter than air, filled with hydrogen, with a steel framework.

Did you know ??????

A **barrage balloon** was a large balloon tethered with metal cables, designed to stop enemy aircraft from approaching. They could also damage the aircraft if it collided with the cables.

◼ Rationing and the effects of submarine warfare

Britain before 1914 had relied on importing food from many parts of the world. With the German U-boat campaign sinking many British ships, the amount of imported food went down and prices went up. Many goods such as sugar, chocolate, cheese, wheat, fruit and butter were in short supply.

For a long time, the government relied on persuading people to eat sensibly and to not waste food. However, in early 1918 the government was forced to introduce some rationing. This included sugar, butter, tea, jam, margarine, meat and bacon. Ration books began to be issued – another development that became much more important in the Second World War. However, in 1918 this was a huge job and it was never finished. Ration books were produced and distributed slowly, but the system had not fully come into operation by the end of the year, even though many poor people wanted it as it was thought to be fair.

◼ The role of women

The war had a major effect on the lives of women. Before the war, some women had been campaigning for women to have the right to vote. Many women had been restricted to looking after the home and bringing up children. The war now brought major opportunities for change.

At first, women took over jobs left by their men. They worked in shops, transport, industries and on the land. In transport women worked on buses and trains as ticket collectors and guards. Some started to drive buses and lorries, or to work as mechanics servicing vehicles. Some worked in banks and post offices. Some worked in agriculture in the Women's Land Army.

However, in Britain the most famous involvement of women was in munitions factories making the shells and bullets needed for fighting. By 1918 nearly 1 million women worked in this dangerous occupation. Many women were nicknamed 'canaries' because the chemicals that they worked with made their skin turn yellow. Working conditions were dangerous and some factories blew up.

However, for this and other demanding jobs, women were much better paid than they had been before the war. A woman working in industry could expect to earn between £3 and £5 a week. Even allowing for inflation during the war, this was a lot of money compared with domestic servants being paid about £2 per month before the war. Many women were becoming more independent of their husbands than before the war. Some began to break free from what they saw as the social restrictions on women that had dominated society. They started to wear trousers and to smoke.

◷◷links

See also 'The role of women in the First World War', page 86.

Did you know ❓❓❓❓❓

The worst munitions factory accident was at Silverton in the East End of London. On 19 January 1917 the factory exploded, killing 69 people and injuring over 400.

Women in the armed forces

From 1917 onwards women also worked in the services. These included the Women's Army Auxiliary Corps (WAAC), the Women's Royal Naval Service (WRNS, often referred to as the Wrens) and the Women's Royal Air Force (WRAF). About 100,000 women did valuable non-fighting jobs in their forces, releasing more men for direct fighting. This again foreshadowed a major development in the Second World War.

From the very start of the war, however, many women volunteered to act as nurses – many in Britain, but increasing numbers abroad. Many bravely worked close to the battle lines treating badly wounded soldiers.

G *Women in an arms factory, c.1915*

Task

3 'Women's lives changed dramatically during the First World War.'

Using Sources **G** and **H** and your own knowledge, explain whether you agree with this interpretation.

H *Volunteer English woman driver washing down her ambulance, a converted Wolseley, donated to the war effort in Cambridge, 1915*

Censorship and propaganda

British censorship

Throughout the war the British government carried out censorship – that is, it limited what the public could learn about the war. The government wanted to keep people patriotic and supporting the war. Therefore, newspapers were not allowed to tell the truth about conditions on the Western Front. Letters from soldiers sent home to families and friends in Britain were also censored. This was done to ensure that, if the letter fell into enemy hands, it would contain no useful information about British positions or future planned movements. British businesses which had foreign trading links also had their correspondence censored.

At first, battles in the war were reported in terms of heroism and victories. Then, when it became impossible to keep up the pretence, in 1916 the government released official film of the Battle of the Somme. The film was shot before and during the battle. The film-makers staged some of the scenes of troops going 'over the top' before the battle started, but then 'real' film was taken of the early stages of the battle. When officials in London saw the volume and quality of the footage taken, the British Committee for War Films decided to make a feature-length film. It lasted just over an hour. It was released in August 1916, while the Battle of the Somme was still going on, first to an invited audience, then in cinemas around the country.

The royal family received a private showing at Windsor Castle in September. Even though it did not show the real extent of the horrors, people were shocked; some fainted. It was intended by the government to spur people in Britain on to even greater efforts. Up to a point it succeeded; it also had the effect of making some people want an immediate end to the slaughter.

Task

4   Investigate more about the use of the silent cinema for propaganda during the First World War.

Task

5   Using Source **I** and your own knowledge, what were the possible advantages of censoring business letters during the First World War?

I *The censorship of business letters. The photo shows commercial letters being examined in 1917*

British propaganda

British propaganda – that is, spreading beliefs and versions of events favourable to Britain – became very well developed. It was evident in newspapers where rumours were accepted as factual stories. For example, British newspapers reported that German soldiers – nicknamed 'the Huns', a barbarian tribe in the Dark Ages – raped nuns and crucified captured enemy soldiers. Photographs were taken and put in newspapers showing proud soldiers returning home and recounting stories of heroism and glory.

Propaganda was evident in the form of posters to encourage the war effort at home – to grow more food, to eat less bread, for women to work in munitions factories or in the countryside. Photographs were published of people happily at work, keen to make any sacrifices needed for Britain to win the war against the evil Germans.

J *British poster encouraging families at home to help the war effort*

6   How effective do you think Source J would be as propaganda during the First World War? Give reasons for your answer.

7   Using the sources provided on the First World War and your own knowledge, what do you think were the most important reasons why British morale on the whole stayed high during the First World War? Explain your answer.

1.2   Britain in the Second World War, 1939–45

Attitudes to war

War started in September 1939. Germany invaded Poland on 1 September; Britain declared war on Germany on 3 September. Almost everyone in Britain accepted that fighting was necessary, but, compared with the First World War, there was little cheering.

Because war had loomed during the spring and summer of 1939, Britain had already begun to make preparations. Gas masks had been issued to every household; plans had been made to deal with air raids. These included blackouts at night; it was an offence to let any light be seen in the street from any buildings.

Unlike the First World War, it was realised that the whole country would be totally involved from the start. Britain could easily be invaded by sea. The German air force could bomb anywhere. Indeed, the air-raid sirens went off in London on 3 September – but it was a false alarm. British people everywhere had to be on high alert.

As the war continued, most people became even more committed to winning, especially when large-scale German bombing started in 1940. As in the First World War, some men registered as conscientious objectors – that is, they refused to fight because of their beliefs. Most of these men helped in the war effort in other ways.

Task

1 Using information from this page and from page 18, including the sources, compare attitudes at the start of the two wars. Why do you think they were so different?

⚭ links

See the Blitz on page 32.

Did you know ??????

Adult gas masks were black, but children's masks were red and blue – they were often called 'Mickey Mouse' masks.

A *The announcement of war, September 1939*

Recruitment and conscription

Immediately the war started, all men aged between 18 and 41 were liable for conscription. The exception was those working in jobs labelled as 'reserved occupations' – that is, jobs that were essential in Britain. Women who were unmarried and over 18 but under 21 had to register for war work or a women's branch of the armed services. Other women, including married ones, were encouraged to volunteer.

Home defence

Air-raid wardens were appointed to ensure blackout regulations were followed and to help during air raids. Many **ARP wardens** were volunteers; some were full-time appointments. During the Blitz many had huge responsibilities in coordinating the movement of people to safety and in cleaning up damage afterwards.

In May 1940 the Local Defence Volunteers, later called the Home Guard, was formed. These local volunteers, up to the age of 65, were intended to provide a line of defence if Britain was invaded. Such was the enthusiasm that 250,000 men signed up in the first seven days and a million and a half by the end of July 1940. Many of the volunteers became impatient that they were not given instant duties, especially as many of them had fought in the First World War. The War Office was too busy at the time to concentrate on them because this was the time when the regular British army was being evacuated from Dunkirk.

They trained in their spare time, even though they had virtually no weapons to begin with. Often they lacked uniforms as well. They trained in the use of weapons, anti-tank warfare (even though weapons were rationed!) and the art of observing and reporting anything suspicious. They acted as lookouts – for example, on the coast to spot an invasion or to catch spies landing under cover of darkness. They guarded important places, such as factories, bridges and railway junctions. Concrete pill boxes, or shelters, were built to house guns and provide cover for Local Defence Volunteers. Barbed wire was spread along the beaches of the south coast. They removed local signposts so that an invading force would get no help in navigating. Blockades were put up at key places to slow down an invading force. The volunteers were at their most active in 1940–41 when the threat of invasion was strongest, but the Home Guard continued its duties until 1944 when the Allies invaded Europe.

It was the sometimes disorganised but totally well-meaning and patriotic nature of the Home Guard that was captured so brilliantly in the 1970s television series *Dad's Army*. The series was funny because of the group of marvellous actors, each representing someone in a society in which everyone knew their position. Hence the pompous bank manager saw himself as a superior to lesser members such as shopkeepers. The scriptwriters often based the episodes on situations and incidents that had actually happened during the war.

Members of the part-time Observer Corps watched the skies to spot enemy aircraft and reported any sightings. Along parts of the English south and east coast the newly invented science of radar could be used to alert Britain of the approach of enemy aircraft over British airspace. Radar's range was extended during the war.

Did you know ??????

The 'reserved occupations' were: dock workers, miners, farmers, scientists, merchant seamen, railway workers and those working in the utilities (water, gas and electricity).

Key terms

ARP warden: Air-raid precaution warden.

B Dad's Army – 1970s British television comedy about the Home Guard during the Second World War

LDV DELAY EXPLAINED –
Call likely at any time

Mr Churchill's announcement yesterday that more than 500,000 men are now enrolled in the Local Defence Volunteers will have surprised many thousands who registered at police stations a month ago and have heard nothing further.

The explanation given by an official at the War Office is that in the majority of cases this apparent neglect is due to the authorized complement [i.e. required number] having been completed.

From the Daily Telegraph, *19 June 1940*

C Delays in processing Local Defence Volunteers

Task

2 How useful is Source **B** for learning about Britain's defence preparations during the Second World War? Use the source and your own knowledge to explain your answer.

Task

3 Look at the explanation given in Source **C** for not recruiting all the volunteers for the Home Guard. This newspaper article was written just after the evacuation of British troops from Dunkirk when the invasion threat was at its worst. What impression does this give of Britain's defence capabilities at the time? Use the source and your own knowledge to explain your answer.

Evacuation

When Hitler took over the rest of Czechoslovakia in March 1939 British people saw that he could not be trusted. He had broken his promise of no more invasions. When the **Nazi–Soviet Pact** was signed on 23 August 1939 the outbreak of war seemed very likely. It was expected that immediately war started there would be large-scale bombing of British cities, especially where important industries were located.

The decision was taken to put into action plans already made to evacuate children. In three days at the beginning of September (just as war was being declared), over 1.5 million children were evacuated from cities to more rural areas. Some went to places quite close to home; some went hundreds of miles away. Some were sent abroad to Canada and other countries in the British Commonwealth.

No bombing happened during the **Phoney War** (September 1939 to May 1940) and gradually children began to return to the cities. After the Battle of Britain (July to September 1940) the Blitz started, with German planes bombing British cities. At that point many children were re-evacuated, not necessarily to the same places. A third evacuation happened in 1944 when German V1 and V2 rocket attacks were launched from northern Europe, affecting parts of south-east England.

Key terms

Nazi–Soviet Pact: the agreement made in August 1939 between Germany and the USSR not to attack each other and to divide Poland between them.

Phoney War: the period in autumn 1939 and spring 1940 when Britain was at war with Germany, but there was no actual fighting.

Task

4   How useful is Source **D** for studying the attitudes of children when they were evacuated from cities in September 1939? Use Source **D** and your own knowledge to explain your answer.

D *An evacuation train leaving the station. Note the children's mixed reactions!*

The treatment of evacuees

When children set out in September 1939, often with their teachers, they were excited about the journey, but perhaps worried about life away from home.

On arrival at their new town or village, they were lined up for host families to choose from. The most scruffy or ill-looking were usually left until last. Some well-off children found themselves living in poor housing with no indoor water supply or toilets. On the other hand some children from very poor slum city backgrounds found themselves living in large mansion houses.

Relations between host families and the evacuees varied enormously. Some hosts only took evacuees out of a sense of duty, or to get them to work on their farm, or for the small allowance paid for having them. Some evacuees were not used to basic hygiene and suffered from head-lice.

On the other hand some host families were delighted with the new members of their family. These evacuees often enjoyed the freedom they gained in the countryside. Some even returned to live and work in the area after the war when they had grown up.

> **❝** *In many cases the children have settled down well and local problems can be cleared up locally. But the problems are very widespread. A very common complaint I hear is about children who have head-lice and, even worse, the children with infectious diseases. One village to my knowledge received 600 Liverpool children of whom no fewer than 485 had such problems.* **❞**
>
> *Written by Kingsley Martin in a London magazine, published 23 September 1939*

E *How evacuees have settled in their new homes*

> **❝** *Jimmy, aged nine, came from London. He was thin, pale and scared. Having fed, scrubbed and de-nitted him, he was less worried. He told us of his exploits at home – street football and fights. Like other city children he knew little about the countryside and was surprised to discover the origins of milk, eggs, bacon and bread.* **❞**
>
> *Margaret Watling, quoted in* Evacuees, M. Brown, 2000

F *A host mother remembers her experiences*

Task

5 'The mass evacuation of children in the Second World War caused more problems than it solved.'

Do you agree with this interpretation? Use Sources **D**, **E** and **F** and your own knowledge to explain your answer.

The Blitz, September 1940 – June 1941

After the failure of the **Battle of Britain** in summer 1940 Hitler changed tactics and ordered the bombing of British cities. The bombing was intended to break the morale of the British people. London was bombed over a period of 77 consecutive nights except one. Many other major cities also suffered much damage, including Liverpool, Plymouth, Southampton, Birmingham and Coventry – all of them ports or centres of industry.

By the time the Blitz ended, about 43,000 people had been killed and 2 million were homeless. However, Britain's morale under the leadership of Prime Minister Winston Churchill had not been broken.

> 66 *As darkness falls, thousands carrying rugs, sandwiches and mattresses go to Central London Tube stations and huddle on the platforms. Here they sit until about 11 pm when they are allowed to lie on the platform and in the passages. They make themselves as comfortable as they can and wait for dawn, playing cards, reading newspapers, talking and sleeping.* 99
>
> *From* News Chronicle, *a British newspaper, 16 September 1940*

G Many Londoners took shelter in underground stations

Task

6 How useful are Sources **G**, **H** and **I** for studying the Blitz? Use the sources and your own knowledge to explain your answer.

H London in ruins, July 1940, when the German Luftwaffe unleashed the Blitz

I A bus in the crater made by a direct Luftwaffe hit on Balham underground station, south London, in October 1940. 64 people were killed and 550 injured

Rationing and the effects of submarine warfare

Only limited amounts of food could be imported because of the submarine warfare in the Atlantic. German U-boats tried to sink as many boats as possible that were bringing supplies to Britain.

Rationing was introduced in January 1940. Ration books containing coupons were issued. Families had to register with a particular shopkeeper and then the shopkeeper received rations according to the number of people who had registered. Butter, sugar and bacon were the first goods to be rationed. Others followed in 1941, such as petrol and clothing.

The government encouraged people to produce more of their own food, using all available land as vegetable gardens or for keeping chickens. The 'Dig for Victory' campaign was very successful, with the number of allotments nearly doubling. Newspaper articles encouraged people to try new recipes. Indeed, many people ate quite healthily during the war, even though some fresh fruits such as oranges, bananas and lemons, were rarely available.

Another way of gaining extra food was through the 'black market'. This was food that had bypassed customs officials and had been smuggled into the country. It was sold at high prices.

Did you know ? ? ? ? ?

The government employed undercover inspectors to make sure that shopkeepers were not illegally selling goods to people without ration coupons.

Task

7   Using Sources **J**, **K** and **L** and your own knowledge, explain how Britain managed to overcome the food blockade of British ports during the Second World War.

J   *Dig for Victory – a famous government poster*

L   *Cooking advice to women facing the effects of rationing*

K   *A government poster encouraging use of vegetables, which could be grown in Britain and were not rationed*

The role of women

From the very beginning of the war, women started to take over jobs left by men. From December 1941 onwards the government said that women between 18 and 40 (except those with young children) had to work in war-related industries. Women in their twenties could be conscripted into the women's armed forces, but not for actual fighting.

There was a shortage of workers on the land, with many men joining the armed forces. About 80,000 women joined the Women's Land Army. Most coped very well with the hard work and were proud of their achievements in helping to feed the population.

Those who were conscripted could join one of three organisations. The Women's Royal Naval Service (WRNS) and the Women's Auxiliary Air Force (WAAF) were the most popular. The Auxiliary Territorial Service (ATS) took most of the conscripts. By 1944 there were 450,000 women working in the three services. Some did essential jobs, including working as mechanics, welders and carpenters. However, many were cooks, cleaners and secretaries.

Women in the home could also play an important part by cooking sensibly, using the suggested recipes published by the government, and trying to make sure that no food was wasted.

∞ links

See also 'The role of women in the Second World War', pages 89–90.

Task

8 'Women were vital in helping Britain win the Second World War.'

Do you agree? Use Sources **M**, **N** and **O** and your own knowledge to explain your answer.

For a healthy, happy job
Join the
WOMEN'S LAND ARMY

For details: CLIVE UPTON
APPLY TO NEAREST W.L.A. COUNTY OFFICE OR TO W.L.A. HEADQUARTERS 6 CHESHAM PLACE LONDON S.W.1
Issued by the Ministry of Agriculture and the Ministry of Labour and National Service

M *A wartime poster about women joining the Land Army*

N *Members of the Women's Land Army harvesting crops, 1940*

O *Women in a tank factory being instructed in the use of a metal power drill, 1940*

Did you know ??????

Some middle-class city women treated the Women's Land Army as a big adventure in the countryside. However, living conditions were very basic. Often there was a shortage of transport with old equipment pressed into use, including horse-drawn ploughs.

Censorship and propaganda

As in the First World War, the government was given special powers by Parliament to control what people could see and hear. The government controlled all films, photographs and written reports. It was assumed that German spies would be reporting any useful information back to Berlin. Censors were allowed to open overseas mail and to tap telephones.

Newsreels had to focus on the positive side of the war – for example, people in London struggling to work after air-raids had destroyed lots of buildings. The names and locations of damaged factories could not be mentioned. Newspapers could not show dead bodies and had to write accounts of campaigns in a way that suggested final victory. The movements of Churchill (Prime Minister from May 1940 onwards) were kept secret. It has been claimed that sometimes when he was allegedly speaking live on the radio to the nation, the voice of an actor was used. This would allow Churchill to move around secretly and reduce the risk of assassination.

Even horoscopes were affected. A government order told newspapers that horoscopes could include details of present difficulties but they had to prophesy that everything would be all right at the end of the war.

The Ministry of Information was the government department responsible for keeping the British public informed about the war and keeping up morale. It published lots of posters. Some early ones were very dull and could be misinterpreted (see Source **P**). Later ones were more eye-catching and could be humorous (see Source **Q**).

Did you know ??????

Norman Shelley, an English actor best known for his work on radio, claimed to have broadcast some speeches for Churchill when he was elsewhere or ill. Whether he did or not, he could certainly imitate Churchill's accent perfectly and after the war did record some of his speeches.

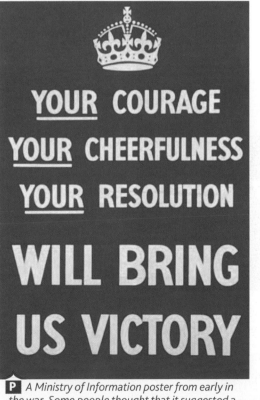

You never know who's listening!

CARELESS TALK COSTS LIVES

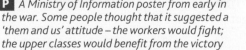

P *A Ministry of Information poster from early in the war. Some people thought that it suggested a 'them and us' attitude – the workers would fight; the upper classes would benefit from the victory*

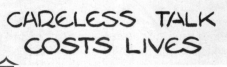

Q *One of a series of cartoons with the same title – 'Careless talk costs lives'*

The development of propaganda techniques

During the war propaganda techniques were developed further. When bad news had to be reported, such as the devastating air-raid attack on Coventry on 15 November 1940, the emphasis was on how inhuman the German bombers were, injuring children, and praising the determination of the people. The *Daily Herald* newspaper reported the next day: 'In every heart there is no fear; only a most passionate hatred of the enemy, and a determination to carry on at all costs'.

Cinemas were the most popular wartime recreation, with up to 30 million tickets sold each week. Each show included two films, a news film and other short reels of information. Therefore, the cinema was an ideal place for propaganda. This was reflected in many of the films, including comedies that made fun of Hitler, such as *The Great Dictator,* starring Charlie Chaplin. Information films could reinforce government regulations about blackouts and food rationing, as well as including heroic stories designed to raise morale.

During the war Abram Games became the country's official war poster designer. He was responsible for many of the most inventive posters that were produced. His motto was 'maximum meaning, minimum means' – in other words, making powerful visual suggestions with only a few words. Below are two examples.

R *Grow your own food*

S *Join the ATS*

Tasks

9   Compare the methods used in Sources **P** and **Q** in order to get a message across. Which do you think is the more effective, and why?

10   Look at Sources **R** and **S**. In each case, how does the artist try to get his propaganda message across?

1 Did the propaganda continue after the war?

After the defeat of Germany, peace was declared in Europe in May 1945. On **VE Day** Prime Minister Winston Churchill spoke to the nation:

'God bless you all. This is your victory! It is the victory of the cause of freedom in every land. In all our long history we have never seen a greater day than this. Everyone, man or woman, has done their best. Everyone has tried. Neither the long years, nor the dangers, nor the fierce attacks of the enemy, have in any way weakened the independent resolve of the British nation.'

You can discuss between yourselves the roles of propaganda in peacetime compared with in times of war. In which areas of life might we admit in Britain that propaganda has an important role in peacetime? Do we call it propaganda? Or is it something that is done to the people of other nations?

Key terms

VE Day: 8 May 1945, the day of victory in Europe for the Allies in World War II.

AQA Controlled Assessment style questions

1 How far do Sources A to F in section 1.1 support the view that everyone in Britain was keen to support their country in the First World War?

You should also use your knowledge of the subject to support your answer.

2 'British women in the Second World War were much more involved in helping to win the war than they had been in the First World War.'

Do you agree with this interpretation?

Use Sources G and H in section 1.1 and Sources M to O in section 1.2 as well as your knowledge of the subject to support your answer.

3 How useful are Sources D to F in section 1.2 for studying the process of evacuation of children from Britain's cities, 1939–40?

Use the sources and your knowledge of the subject to support your answer.

4 'Propaganda affected people's lives much more in the Second World War than in the First World War.'

Do you agree with this interpretation?

Use Sources I and J in section 1.1 and Sources P to S in section 1.2 as well as your knowledge of the subject to support your answer.

2.1 The war on land

 A *The Western Front 1914–18*

Objectives

In this chapter you will learn about:

the methods of warfare used in the First and Second World Wars

how far these methods were similar and how far they were different

why Britain and her allies were victorious in both World Wars

developing skills of source evaluation to test the reliability, utility and accuracy of evidence

evaluating a number of sources to test an interpretation.

First World War

When the First World War broke out in August 1914, most people expected that it would be over by Christmas. The Germans attacked Belgium using the Schlieffen Plan, but were delayed by the resistance of the Belgians and the British Expeditionary Force (BEF) and stopped at the Battle of the Marne. The Germans retreated and began to dig trenches. The war of movement was over and gave way to trench warfare. Both sides dug in and faced each other in trenches across the Western Front. In between them lay 'no man's land'. There were major battles, especially at Verdun, the Somme and Passchendaele, which cost thousands of lives as each side tried to break through the other's trenches. The trenches went from the Channel to the Swiss border and the front did not move more than a few miles until the German defeat in 1918.

Task

1 How useful are Sources **A** and **B** in explaining why the First World War was not over by Christmas 1914?

B *British troops digging in Flanders on the Western Front*

Trench warfare

The invention of the machine gun changed the whole idea of fighting. Cavalry charges were useless against the rapid fire of the machine gun. New tactics had to be developed. The British generals were convinced that the only way to win the war was to capture the trenches of the enemy and force them to surrender. This led to a series of attacks on the opposition trenches. All the attacks followed the same pattern. They would begin with a bombardment of the German trenches using the heavy artillery. This was intended to break up the barbed wire which defended the trenches, and destroy the machine gun posts. The men would then be ordered to advance towards the enemy trenches. They would go 'over the top' of the trenches, walk across no man's land and capture the opposition trenches.

C The 1998 London production of Journey's End. The play was written in 1928 by English playwright R.C. Sherriff. It was first produced in 1928 and is based on Sherriff's own experience as a captain in the East Surrey Regiment. It takes place in a dugout near St Quentin in March 1918, just before the last great German offensive, as the soldiers prepare to go 'over the top' in a daytime mission

> 66 *Crowds of men were crouching round, heating up their canteens of water, some frying pieces of meat, others heating soup, and all the time laughing and talking. From other groups came the quiet humming of favourite songs … And these men knew they were going over the top in the morning. They knew that many would not be alive tomorrow night, yet I never saw a sad face, nor heard a word of complaint.* 99

Geoffrey Malins, quoted in Britain and the Great War, G. Hetherton, 1998

D An official government photographer describes the night before the start of the Battle of the Somme

In reality, the bombardment did not destroy the machine gun posts, which were protected by concrete defences, and the wire remained uncut so the soldiers had to stop to cut their way through it. This made them sitting targets for the German machine guns. The ground had been churned up by the bombardment which made it difficult to walk over. These offensives lasted for months, but little ground was gained and many lives were lost. This type of warfare is known as a war of attrition. It was an attempt to wear down the opposition and weaken their morale.

Task

2 a What impression is given in Sources **C** and **D** of the feeling of soldiers who are going 'over the top'? Notice their facial expressions.

b Why do you think the two sources are different?

c How useful are sources like these in informing you about the attitudes of soldiers to trench warfare?

Conditions in the trenches

The soldiers lived in dreadful conditions in the trenches. The heavy rain led to water lining the floor of the trench. Standing in the water for long periods of time caused the soldiers to develop a painful swelling of the toes called 'trench foot'. Food was normally limited to bully beef with a biscuit and jam. Washing was difficult and the men were often infested with lice. The damp and the dead bodies attracted rats which disturbed the men's sleep at night. The worst thing was fear of death. If a man stuck his head over the edge of the trench he could be shot by a sniper; if the soldiers were ordered to go 'over the top', they knew many of them would not return. The days were long and boring as the men waited for an attack. The nights were often spent checking the barbed wire defences to make sure there were no gaps in them.

> 66 *Oh, how I long for this to end quickly and to be able to get to my dear home and loved ones. Times are cruel and hard and even the weather has no mercy for us. It has snowed, hailed and rained in torrents daily. For the past two months I have had soaked feet and clothes. I have never had my clothes off – everything has to dry on us. I have absolutely no feeling in my feet and hands. We stand, lie and sit in mud and water.* 99
>
> *Quoted in* Britain and the World, *T. and S. Lancaster, 2004*

E *Letter from Lance Corporal Matthews to his wife written in April 1917. Matthews was killed in May 1917*

F *War trenches in 1916*

Did you know ??????

Trench foot was caused by the combination of cold, damp weather and constricting shoes. It caused feet to become numb and turn red or blue, as well as causing blisters and fungal infections. If it was not treated it could lead to gangrene, which might result in amputation.

Did you know ??????

The term 'bully beef' comes from the French *bouilli*, meaning 'boiled'.

Did you know ??????

Early in the war, German snipers were very effective as a result of the high quality lenses the Germans were able to manufacture. It was not until later in the war that the British developed the same technology. The British also trained their snipers in special sniper schools.

Tasks

3   How do Sources **E** and **F** help us to understand conditions in the trenches?

4   How reliable is the description of conditions in the trenches in Source **E**?

New technology in warfare

The machine gun was the most effective weapon on the Western Front at the beginning of the war, but it was mainly a defensive weapon. When used by the opposition it made it virtually impossible to take the enemy's trenches and led to the stalemate that lasted until 1918. Various weapons were introduced in an attempt to break this stalemate. In 1915 the Germans used gas. It surprised the British and the Germans did make advances, but these were short-lived because the wind changed direction and blew the gas towards the German trenches. More lethal gases were developed and used, such as mustard gas, which could blind and kill people, in serious cases, and could also contaminate a soldier's uniform and equipment and infect anyone who came into contact with them. Similarly they could also be absorbed through the skin, which meant that gas masks were ineffective as protection. However, the effects of gas were limited. Gas masks were issued to all soldiers, but the main effect was psychological – soldiers feared the prospects of being gassed more than the actual effects.

G *British gas casualties, April 1918*

The British introduced tanks at the Battle of the Somme in 1916. The Germans were surprised by the size and strength of the tanks and retreated, but the tanks were unreliable and many broke down or got stuck in the mud. They were more successful in 1918 and played a large part in the allied advance and final defeat of Germany.

Opinions differed on the usefulness of tanks

> A pretty mechanical toy but of very limited military value.

H Lord Kitchener's view of the tank in 1915

> It was a mistake to put them into the battle of the Somme. They will have to penetrate a terrific artillery barrage, and will have to operate in broken country full of shell craters.

Quoted in Purnell's History of the Twentieth Century, *1971*

I Prime Minister Asquith on the tank in September 1916

> It was marvellous. The tank waddled on with its guns blazing and we could see Jerry popping up and down, not knowing what to do, whether to stay or run. The Jerries waited until our tank was only a few yards away and then fled. The tank just shot them down and the machine gun post, the gun itself, the dead and wounded who had not been able to run, just disappeared. The tank went right over them.

From The Somme, L. MacDonald, *1993*

J Description of the work of a tank in the Battle of the Somme by an eyewitness, Lance Corporal Len Lovell

> When the German troops crept out of their dugouts in the midst of the morning and stretched their necks to look for the English, their blood chilled. Mysterious monsters were crawling towards them over the craters. Nothing stopped them. Someone in the trenches said, 'The devil is coming', and word was passed along the line. Tongues of flame leapt from the sides of the iron caterpillars. The English infantry came in behind.

K A German war correspondent describes the effect of tanks on the Germans at the Somme

Did you know ??????

As Secretary of State for War, Lord Kitchener made many contributions to Britain's war effort both in a military capacity and on the home front. He was involved in the development of a new pattern for knitting socks with a seamless join of the toe to prevent rubbing, known as the Kitchener stitch!

Did you know ??????

The nickname 'Jerry' was given to German soldiers during the First World War. It is likely that it originates from the word 'German', but could also have come from the shape of a German helmet which looked like a chamber pot. The British were known as 'Tommy'. These nicknames were the origin of the characters in the well-known cartoon, Tom and Jerry!

Tasks

5 How do Sources **G** and **K** help us to understand the effect of weapons such as gas and tanks on the opposition soldiers?

6 Do Sources **J** to **M** support the views of the tank given in Sources **H** and **I**? Explain your answer.

L *Allied tanks capture German trenches, July 1918*

" HIMMEL ! THE ALL-HIGHEST HAS THE TRUTH SPOKEN—THE WORST IS BEHIND US."

M *Allied tanks chasing the German army. A cartoon from* Punch *magazine, 21 August 1918*

The Second World War

Blitzkrieg

The Second World War broke out in September 1939 when Germany and the USSR attacked Poland. Britain's active part in the war only began in April 1940 when Hitler attacked Norway. Norway was taken by the Germans and Prime Minister Chamberlain was forced to resign by members of the government who wanted Britain to take a more active role. He was replaced by Winston Churchill. In May German troops attacked France through Belgium. As in the First World War, the British sent the BEF to defend France, but with little success. Improvements in tanks and aircraft led to Germany using a new type of warfare called 'Blitzkrieg' or lightning war.

Blitzkrieg involved the use of aircraft, tanks and infantry in combination. It would begin with a bombardment to weaken the enemy. Aircraft, often dive bombers, would then bomb enemy headquarters and key positions behind the front line. Soldiers were landed behind the lines by plane and gliders. The main attack came from groups of tanks supported by infantry in trucks which would attack weak points in the defence line. The surprise and speed of the attack enabled the Germans to break through and quickly defeat the French. The BEF was in danger of being stranded in France, so they were ordered to evacuate from Dunkirk at the end of May 1940.

N *The evacuation from Dunkirk*

Evacuation from Dunkirk, 1940

The evacuation from Dunkirk (Operation Dynamo) began on
27 May 1940 and lasted for 9 days until 4 June. Almost 700 boats
were involved in taking the men from the beaches at Dunkirk. Most
of them came home in merchant ships and destroyers, but a variety of
boats were involved including trawlers, lifeboats, paddle steamers and
pleasure craft. A few of these carried men back to Britain, but mostly
the smaller boats collected the men from the beaches and took them to
the larger boats which were anchored further offshore. Over 338,000
men were rescued including about 140,000 French.

The beaches were attacked by German planes, but Hitler decided to
halt his forces to wait for further supplies. He appeared to be confident
of victory and wanted to save his tanks for the attack on Paris. Goering,
the commander of the German air force, had convinced Hitler that the
air force could destroy the retreating British forces. Groups of soldiers,
many of them French, defended the beaches until the boats had left
and then gave themselves up and became prisoners of war.

Altogether there were almost 70,000 British casualties and the British
troops had to leave all their equipment including field guns and armed
vehicles. They also lost six destroyers, 24 small warships and about
70 little ships. But the evacuation was seen as a great victory because
the British government only expected to rescue 40,000 men at the
most. Moreover, the rescued men could form the basis of the new
army. However, the BEF had failed in its mission to protect France.
The French had been abandoned and felt betrayed by Britain. German
troops occupied Paris on 14 June and the French accepted peace terms
on 22 June. Although Churchill told the House of Commons 'Wars are
not won by evacuations', the press greeted the rescue as the 'Miracle of
Dunkirk.'

> **Did you know** ??????
>
> Codenames were used by
> governments and military
> commanders to protect the
> secrecy of military operations
> for communications purposes.
> Operation Dynamo took its name
> from the dynamo room in the
> naval headquarters below Dover
> Castle, where the operation was
> planned.

Dunkirk, 1940

Views on the evacuation

> 66 An artillery man told me that with thousands of others he had spent two days among the sand dunes with little food and no shelter from the German dive bombers. Yet the men still joked, played cards, and even started a football game to keep up their spirits ... A sailor told me that a vessel in which he had been assisting on the Belgian coast had been sunk. No sooner had he and his comrades landed in England than they all volunteered to go back at once. 99
>
> *From the* Daily Mail, *1 June 1940*

P *Interviews with two evacuees from Dunkirk*

> 66 The evacuation has been overglamourised. Reports of 'merciless bombing' and 'the hell of Dunkirk' were ridiculous. I walked along the beaches on several occasions and never saw a corpse; there was little shelling. 99
>
> *From the* Green Howards Gazette, *November 1962*

Q *View on the evacuation by General Franklyn, a divisional commander at Dunkirk, writing in 1962*

> 66 I hated Dunkirk. It was just cold-blooded killing. The beaches were jammed with soldiers. I went up and down spraying them with bullets. 99
>
> *Quoted in* The Second World War, *C.K. MacDonald, 1984*

R *From a letter home, written by a German fighter pilot in 1940*

Tasks

7 What impression of the evacuation from Dunkirk is given by Sources **N** to **P**?

8 a How do Sources **Q** and **R** differ in their accounts of Dunkirk?

  b Why do you think they are different?

D-Day, 1944

After their defeat of France in 1940, the Germans occupied the whole of Northern France and the Atlantic coast. Operation Overlord was the Allied planned attack to free France from German occupation in 1944. Hitler was expecting the attack, but he did not know where the allies would land in France. The Allied commander-in-chief, the American General Eisenhower, ordered air attacks to be made on Calais and this convinced the Germans that the attack would take place there. In fact, when the attack came it was in Normandy which gave some element of surprise. The landings in Normandy took place over five beaches and resistance was different on each of them.

On 6 June 1944 planes and gliders dropped paratroops into Normandy to destroy some German defences and to interrupt their lines of communication. This was followed by a vast fleet of about 4,000 ships which landed over 120,000 soldiers on the beaches on 6 June (D-Day). The invading soldiers brought their own artificial harbours, called 'mulberries', to enable them to land troops and equipment. The five beaches were codenamed Utah, Omaha, Gold, Juno and Sword going from west to east and were between Cherbourg and Caen. The Americans landed on the first two, the British and Canadians on the other three. Fighting was fiercest on Omaha and the Americans lost over 3,000 men in seizing the beach. A foothold was established in Northern France, but Germany refused to surrender. The Allied forces continued to advance and Germany finally gave up in May 1945.

Did you know ??????

The term D-Day is a general military term used to explain the day on which an operation will take place. The initial 'D' comes from the word 'day'. The term 'D-Day' has been used for many different operations, but it is now generally only used to refer to the Allied landings in Normandy on 6 June 1944 in the Second World War.

S *American forces on D-Day*

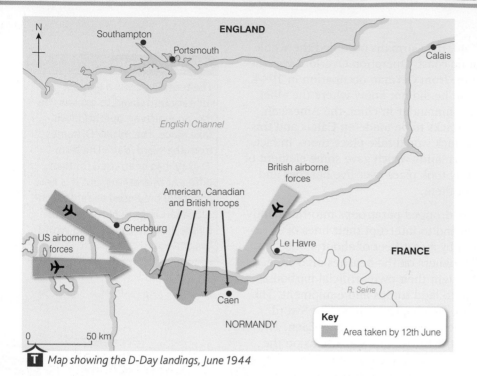

T Map showing the D-Day landings, June 1944

U An American reporter describes the scene at D-Day

V US army report on the landings at Omaha

Tasks

9 What can we learn about the D-Day landings from Sources **S** and **T**?

10 Sources **U** and **V** are both describing the scene on 6 June 1944. Why are they different?

2.2 The war at sea

First World War

The main duty of the British navy during the First World War was to protect Britain from attack by the German High Seas Fleet. German raiders attacked towns on the east coast of England in 1914 but early skirmishes in the North Sea at Heligoland and the Dogger Bank confirmed the supremacy of the British fleet. It was able to ensure safe passage of supplies to the army in France and began the blockade of German ports. The only major sea battle of the war was at Jutland in 1916.

Jutland, 1916

Both sides claimed victory in this battle. Britain lost 14 ships and 6,000 men whereas the Germans only lost 11 ships and 2,500 men. Moreover, the British had managed to trap the Germans at Jutland and then allowed them to escape through the mist.

> **Did you know** ??????
>
> The German High Seas Fleet or *Hochseeflotte* was the main battle fleet of the Imperial German Navy during the First World War. It posed such a threat to the Royal Navy's control of the seas around Britain that the British navy was forced to remain concentrated in the North Sea for most of the war, seriously weakening Britain's military power.

> 66 At Jutland, the German fleet was no longer fit for battle and could only make for harbour and repairs. The British fleet remained largely intact and ready to renew the fight. The German fleet would not risk another encounter with the British fleet and the morale of the fleet lowered through inactivity. In 1917 there was a mutiny in the German fleet which was put down, but when ordered to put to sea in 1918, it revolted which spread and led to the final surrender of Germany. This is perhaps the most important result of the battle of Jutland. 99
>
> Captain D. Macintyre, quoted in Purnell's History of the Twentieth Century, 1971

A *Jutland – a British view*

> **Did you know** ??????
>
> Heligoland was the first naval battle of the First World War, fought on 28 August 1914, after the British planned to attack German fleets off the north-west coast of Germany.

> 66 After Jutland, the tactical advantage was with the High Seas Fleet. They had inflicted about double their own losses on a greatly superior opponent. The fleet was proud of this achievement. Their main duty after Jutland was to support the submarine war and to provide its best young officers to the submarines. The break up of the fleet in 1918 was due to malnutrition and the hopeless military position of Germany. 99
>
> Vice Admiral F. Ruge, quoted in Purnell's History of the Twentieth Century, 1971

B *Jutland – a German view*

Task

1. Explain the arguments used in Sources **A** and **B**. What evidence is there to support them?

The British blockade of Germany

From 1914 the British fleet tried to prevent any goods reaching Germany in an attempt to starve Germany into defeat. They did this by searching all ships going to Germany and seized any goods on them. They mined international waters to stop German ships entering large sections of sea. The battle of Jutland was an attempt to break this blockade, but it failed. By 1916 German harvests were beginning to fail because of the lack of imported fertilisers and because of severe frosts which affected the year's potato crop. Malnutrition caused by lack of food led to a lowering of morale in Germany. The shortage of clothing was increasing and food was so scarce in Germany in 1917 that it became known as the 'turnip winter'. In 1918 an epidemic of deadly flu, often referred to as Spanish flu, broke out killing many and weakening Germany further. Deaths from disease increased and led to widespread opposition to the government, and ultimately to the final surrender of Germany.

Submarine warfare

The Germans attempted to blockade Britain using their U-boats (submarines). In 1915 the Germans introduced unrestricted submarine warfare. This meant that they would attack any ships including neutral vessels which were in the seas around Britain. In this way they hoped to cut off all food supplies bound for Britain. This policy brought protests from neutral countries and when Americans were killed on board the British liner *Lusitania* in 1915, Germany called off unrestricted submarine warfare until 1917. The *Lusitania* was a passenger liner not a military boat. Its sinking provoked hostility among many neutral countries, particularly the USA. The recent discovery of munitions in the wreck indicates it may have been a blockade runner, and therefore a legitimate target. When unrestricted submarine warfare was resumed in 1917, it brought the USA into the war and Britain to within six weeks of starvation.

Britain survived unrestricted submarine warfare because of the extra measures taken to defend against the U-boats. A system of mines and submarine nets was set up round the Straits of Dover and other areas surrounding Britain. Destroyers disguised as merchant ships (Q ships) made attacks on shipping more dangerous for the U-boats, and aircraft began to be used for spotting the position of the submarines. Q ships patrolled areas of the sea and were usually small and unimpressive boats so that the U-boats would not see them as a threat. They were regularly repainted, refitted and had their flags changed overnight so that they looked different.

The most effective defence against U-boats was the armed convoy. Merchant vessels began to sail in groups protected by armed destroyers. One slow-moving merchant ship was an easy prey for the submarines, but it was more difficult for them to attack a group, especially when the merchant ships were protected by faster-moving destroyers which could pursue the submarines and use depth charges to destroy them.

Did you know ??????

The 1918 flu epidemic, often called the Spanish flu, spread to nearly every part of the world. The exact number of people killed by the flu is unknown but it is estimated to be double the number of people killed in the First World War itself. Although the war didn't cause the epidemic, troop movements and the fact that soldiers lived in such close quarters in the trenches certainly helped to spread the virus.

Did you know ??????

The crews of Q ships had to look like ordinary merchant seamen rather than naval officers, and some even dressed as women to fool the enemy!

C *German submarines sunk 1914–18*

Method of sinking	1914–16	1917–18
Rammed	2	8
By patrol vessels	15	40
By Q ships	5	6
By convoy escorts	0	16
By mines	10	38

D *Tonnage (in millions) of British shipping lost to U-boats*

1914–16	1917	1918
2	3.5	1.5

Second World War

Naval strategy in the Second World War was similar to that used in the First World War. Britain had to try to keep supply routes open, to protect the coastline from attack and to place a blockade on Germany. The German navy was of little danger to the British fleet, especially after the destruction of the German battleships, *Graf Spee* (1939), *Bismarck* (1941) and *Tirpitz* (1944). Routes in the Mediterranean were kept open by the defeat of the Italian navy at Cape Matapan in 1941.

The Battle of the Atlantic

As in the First World War, the main danger to Britain was the U-boat. Unrestricted submarine warfare was introduced immediately by the Germans and attacks on supplies coming to Britain took place. The strategy was the same, but the struggle was different because of developments in technology between the wars. Britain used convoys from the beginning, but the German tactics of hunting in groups of submarines, called 'wolfpacks', made convoys less successful than in the First World War. Hitler's conquest of France and Norway gave Germany the use of French and Norwegian ports, so their U-boats could stay in the Atlantic for longer and would have greater air support from the German air force. This made Britain even more vulnerable than in the First World War and the years 1940 to 1943 were referred to as the 'happy time' by the U-boats.

Tasks

2   Study Sources **C** and **D**. Which was the most successful weapon against the U-boat?

3   Germany had more U-boats at sea in 1918 than any other year of the war. Explain why they were less successful in 1918.

The defeat of the U-boats

The U-boats nearly succeeded. In January 1943 the British navy only had two months' supply of oil left. The combination of the entry of the USA into the war in 1941 and improved technology, came to Britain's aid. American ships helped to protect the convoys and by 1943 more ships were being produced than the number destroyed by U-boats. Special anti-submarine frigates were developed which prevented the submarines from surfacing. Depth charges were made more effective and the 'asdic' sonar device enabled submarines to be accurately located under water.

Long-distance 'Liberator' bombers were used to protect the convoys. These could cover the whole of the Atlantic, giving shipping greater protection. Submarines could not stay under water all the time and had to surface for air. They did this normally at night when they could not be seen. Improvements in radar meant that devices were now small enough to be fitted to aircraft which could use them along with searchlights (the Leigh Light) to spot U-boats at night and to identify their exact position. The Germans were losing too many submarines, and fortunes in the Battle of the Atlantic were changing.

E *The Battle of the Atlantic*

Year	U-boat losses	British and American losses (millions of tons)	British and American new construction (millions of tons)
1939	9	0.8	0.3
1940	22	4.5	1
1941	35	4.4	2
1942	85	8	7
1943	287	3.5	14
1944	241	1.4	13
1945	153	0.45	4

F *The sinking of a British cargo ship by a submarine*

Tasks

4 How useful are Sources **E** and **F** to an historian writing about the Battle of the Atlantic?

5 What were the main differences between the war at sea in the First and Second World Wars?

2.3 | The war in the air

First World War

Aircraft were not seen as important assets in warfare in 1914. It was only when the stalemate of the trenches occurred that their possibilities were seen, improvements made and they were used in wider roles. In 1914 Britain only had 119 aircraft; in 1918 they had over 3,000. The planes of 1914 were mostly biplanes made of wood and canvas held together with piano wire and had a top speed of about 60 miles per hour. The pilots wore goggles and thick jackets to protect them from the wind and cold.

In 1914 the British used their planes to spot enemy positions and movements both on the Western Front and at sea. As the war went on, it was realised that the planes could be used to much greater effect to engage with enemy aircraft. As a result, they were fitted with machine guns which enabled fights between aircraft in the sky known as 'dogfights'. The Air Aces who fought in these became heroes and received much publicity, probably to distract people from the deaths in the trenches. Men such as Mick Mannock, Albert Ball and Billy Bishop became household names in Britain, as did Manfred von Richthofen, the Red Baron, and Hermann Goering in Germany. Planes also dropped bombs by hand on the trenches and were fired at by the soldiers in the trench. In 1918 the British used planes to hold up the last offensive of the Germans by firing at the troops from the sky.

The Germans thought that they could bomb Britain into submission by using airships called Zeppelins to reduce the morale of civilians. These airships were very fast and could carry more guns and bombs than other similar aircraft of the time. They did have a disadvantage: they were vulnerable to gunfire attacks from the ground and from other aircraft, which meant they could not be used effectively in daytime raids. There were over 50 Zeppelin raids on Britain, mostly at night, causing more than 1,000 casualties and some damage to property, but the British had aircraft which were able to intercept the Zeppelins and used searchlights to identify their position.

More successful were the German planes which began regular bombing raids on London in 1917. Civilians were now in danger and the aeroplane could be seen as a frightening new weapon. By the time the war ended, Britain had plans in place for bombing attacks on Berlin.

The future for war in the air

During the First World War, the function of aircraft was essentially to support the army and navy through reconnaissance. The decisive role in winning the war came from the army and navy. Technology had advanced quickly during the war. Developments in the speed, strength and mechanism of the aircraft widened their use. In 1914 the British air force had been split between the Royal Flying Corps and the Royal Naval Service. In 1918 these two forces became the Royal Air Force. People were beginning to realise the possibility that aircraft could win a future war on their own.

> **Did you know** ??????
>
> The term 'Ace' was initially used by the French in reference to a pilot who had shot down five enemy planes. The individual British squadrons of the RAF certainly kept scores, and after 1916, a pilot who had achieved five 'decisive' victories in air combat was usually guaranteed to receive a Military Cross for his actions.

∞links

For more details about the German Zeppelin raids look back to page 22.

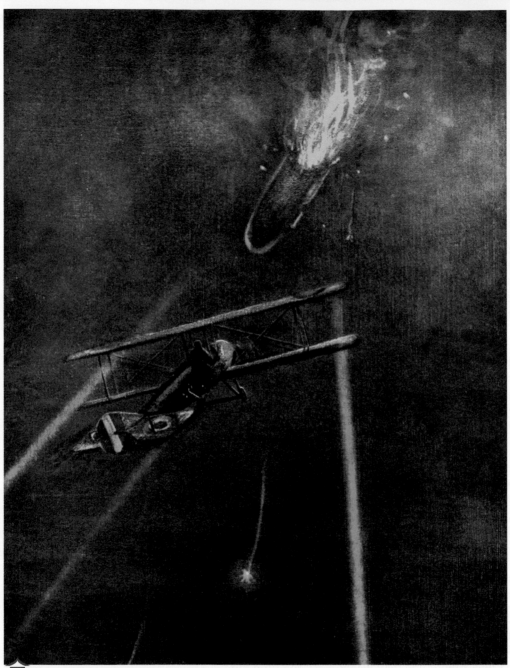

A *Illustration produced in 1920 showing a Zeppelin airship being shot down over London in 1916*

Second World War

Advances in aircraft design and weaponry increased their use in the Second World War. Aircraft played a more important role in the support of ground troops and protection of shipping and were able to play a part in transporting forces to positions behind the enemy lines. In the early years of the war, the German blitzkrieg tactics used aircraft to support the infantry in their attack. In 1944 the D-Day campaign began with planes landing troops behind enemy lines. Air Aces of the Second World War such as Douglas Bader were popularised by the media as they had been in the First World War.

∞ links

For details on the war at sea, see page 49, for more on blitzkrieg, see page 44, for D-Day, page 47.

Task

1 What can you learn from Source **A** about the war in the air during the First World War?

The Battle of Britain

After he had defeated France, Hitler tried to make peace with Britain, but Prime Minister Winston Churchill refused, so Hitler set about planning an invasion of Britain (Operation Sealion). In order to get his forces safely across the Channel, Hitler had to win control of the skies. In August 1940 the German air force, the *Luftwaffe*, set about the destruction of the RAF. The Luftwaffe attacked radar installations, aircraft factories and airfields. Hundreds of German aircraft took off from airfields in France each day. Bombers were accompanied by Messerschmitt fighter planes. Warned by radar that they were coming, British fighter planes (Hurricanes and Spitfires) went into the air to meet them. Dogfights took place and losses were severe. Britain was saved on 7 September 1940 when Hitler changed tactics. He stopped attacking airfields and ordered the bombing of London. This was a crucial mistake which gave Britain the opportunity to repair the airfields and replace the lost planes.

The Blitz

The failure of the Luftwaffe to destroy the RAF led to Hitler calling off Operation Sealion in September 1940. The purpose of the Blitz was to bomb Britain into defeat. The idea was to target factories and transport networks so that Britain could not continue the war. The attacks on cities would affect civilians and reduce their morale and their willingness to continue the fight.

London was bombed regularly as were other industrial centres and ports such as Plymouth, Southampton, Birmingham, Coventry and Manchester. In spite of the damage and destruction, Britain did not give in. By the summer of 1941, Hitler had made another vital decision: Germany attacked Soviet Russia. The Blitz was over.

∞ links

For more details on the Blitz, see page 32.

B *Dornier bombers in the Blitz, 1940*

The bombing of Germany

As well as defending Britain, the RAF also played an offensive role in the war. British bombing attacks on Germany started in 1940 with attacks on roads and communications. This was followed by attacks on German industry and military establishments. From the beginning of 1942 the raids became more general and appeared to be aimed more at reducing the morale of the German citizens, especially the industrial workers, so that the German war effort would be affected. Many of these early British bombing raids were unsuccessful. Daytime attacks were dangerous and resulted in heavy British casualties, night-time attacks were often unsuccessful and missed their targets.

When Sir Arthur Harris was appointed to Bomber Command in 1942, tactics changed. The RAF began 'area bombing' Germany. Harris appeared convinced that Germany could be bombed into surrender. In May 1942 came the first 1,000-strong bomber raid on Cologne. When the USA entered the war in 1941 they launched daylight attacks on Germany from bases in Britain. The formation of the Pathfinder force in 1943, made up of elite crew, improved the accuracy of the raids. In the 'Dambusters' raid of 1943, two dams on the Ruhr were breached by special bouncing bombs and the surrounding area flooded, but even in this, a third dam remained firm and eight British bombers were destroyed.

Task

2 How do Sources **B** and **C** help us to understand the war in the air in the Second World War?

Did you know ??????

Sir Arthur Harris was known as 'Bomber' Harris by the press, and even 'Butcher' Harris in the RAF itself. He improved standards of instruction and training and made British aerial tactics much more ruthless and efficient.

C Bombers over Germany, September 1943

By 1943 cities of Germany were being bombed every hour of the day. In that year came the first fire bomb attacks directed at Hamburg. Around 50,000 people were killed, even more fled from the city and over 80 bombers were shot down. Similar raids were tried on Berlin but they did not create the same fires and too many planes were lost. Large numbers of citizens were killed or left homeless. In 1945 when Germany was on the brink of defeat, the RAF bombed Dresden destroying most of the city and killing thousands of civilians. German morale did not crack, but many argue that the main effect of the bombing campaigns was that it diverted German planes and guns from the Eastern Front and enabled the USSR to advance more quickly into Germany.

Allied bombers also played an important part in the D-Day invasion of France in 1944. They bombed the railways and communication systems of France and Belgium to hinder the German attempts to bring up reinforcements to defend their position in France. They had to be accurate raids because otherwise they risked killing citizens of 'friendly' countries (France and Belgium). The targets were marked out by master bombers, the most famous of whom was Leonard Cheshire who was awarded the Victoria Cross for his bravery and outstanding courage over a period of time.

V1 and V2

Towards the end of the war, London was terrified by attacks from flying bombs known as 'doodlebugs'. Although they were very dangerous, the British were able to develop some protection from them by locating anti-aircraft guns nearer to coastal areas so as to be able to shoot them down away from urban areas where they would cause the most damage. More dangerous were the V2 rockets. There was no defence against these and they came silently. Fortunately for Britain, the capture of the launching sites in Belgium and Holland removed their threat.

> **Did you know** ??????
>
> In 1959, Leonard Cheshire and his wife Sue Ryder formed homes to care for the disabled and severely ill people. These homes are still named after them to this day.

> **Did you know** ??????
>
> The German V1 bomb was also known as a 'doodlebug'. The name comes from an Australian insect, which makes a loud buzzing noise like the V1 bomb.

D *Bombing in the Second World War*

	Bombs dropped on Germany in tons	Bombs dropped on Britain in tons
1940	10,000	36,000
1941	30,000	22,000
1942	40,000	3,000
1943	120,000	2,000
1944	650,000	9,000
1945	500,000	800

E *German output in the Second World War*

	Coal and steel (millions of tons)		Tanks	Aircraft
1940	268	21	2,200	10,200
1941	315	28	5,200	11,800
1942	318	29	9,200	15,400
1943	340	31	17,300	24,800
1944	348	26	22,100	39,800

> **Task**
>
> **3** How useful are Sources **D** and **E** in helping us to explain the effects of the Allied bombing of Germany?

Why were Britain and her allies victorious in the two World Wars?

First World War

There are several reasons why Germany lost this war. The main ones are summarised below. They need to be explained using the earlier parts of this chapter.

- Germany needed a quick victory. Once the Schlieffen Plan failed, the German economy and army could not cope with a war on two fronts.
- Allied sea power, particularly the British navy, was decisive in the final defeat of Germany.
- The entry of the USA and its vast resources were decisive.

Second World War

This war was fought over a greater area than the First World War and over more fronts. The main reasons for the defeat of Germany are summarised below.

- Hitler's mistake of failing to defeat Britain both at Dunkirk and in the Battle of Britain. This allowed Britain to become the base for the freeing of Europe from Nazi control.
- The Allies built up naval supremacy which enabled them to win the Battle of the Atlantic and keep supply routes to Europe open.
- The air superiority gained by the Allies was vital in winning the war.
- Hitler tried to achieve too much and overstretched Germany's resources which could not match the combined resources of the USA and the USSR.

AQA Controlled Assessment style questions

1   Study Sources C to F in section 2.1.

Explain how useful these sources are to you in understanding the nature of trench warfare in the First World War.

2   Study Sources H to M in section 2.1.

Explain how useful these sources are in showing you the attitude to and effect of the introduction of new weapons in the First World War.

3   Study Sources N to R in section 2.1.

Explain how useful these sources are in understanding what happened at Dunkirk in 1940.

4   'The greatest contribution of the Royal Navy in both World Wars was its victory over the German U-boats.'

How far do Sources A to F in section 2.2 support this interpretation of the contribution of the Royal Navy to the wars? You should also use your knowledge of the subject to support your answer.

5   'The main role of the British air force in the First World War was to defend Britain, whereas its main role in the Second World War was to defeat Germany.'

How far do Sources A to E in section 2.3 support this interpretation of the changing role of the British air force in the two World Wars? You should also use your knowledge of the subject to support your answer.

3.1 Britain in the 1920s and 1930s

A 'The Solidarity of Labour' from Punch, May 1921

Objectives

In this chapter you will learn about:

the impact of two World Wars on British society

how far the 1920s and 1930s was a period of industrial unrest and economic depression in Britain

the reconstruction of Britain in the late 1940s and 1950s and how it changed Britain

developing skills of source evaluation to test the reliability, utility and accuracy of evidence

evaluating a number of sources to test an interpretation.

■ Economic problems resulting from the aftermath of war

Lloyd George, the British Prime Minister, had promised a 'land fit for heroes' in the 1918 election campaign. People expected the government to introduce reforms in, for example, education, housing and national insurance, and to create jobs. Instead Britain faced new economic problems. British markets overseas had been lost in the war and were not recovered after it. New industrial powers, especially the USA and Japan, had captured British markets. This led to poor industrial relations and strikes – especially in the coal industry.

The mining industry had been controlled by the government during the war. In 1921 pits were returned to their owners. The mine owners immediately reduced wages. This led to the threat of a major strike involving miners, transport workers and railwaymen – the **Triple Alliance**. However, on Black Friday, April 1921, the other two unions backed away from strike action. The miners were forced to accept a wage cut.

The General Strike, 1926

The causes of the General Strike lay in the mining industry. In 1925 mine owners tried to reduce wages and to lengthen the working day. The government set up the Samuel Commission to look into the mining industry and subsidised miners' wages. The Samuel Commission published its report in March 1926. It recognised that the industry needed to be reorganised but opposed the idea of nationalisation. The report also recommended that the government subsidy should be ended and that miners' wages should be reduced. In 1926 the subsidy ended with the Commission failing to solve the problems. Miners' wages were cut. The Trade Union Congress (TUC), the body representing trade unions, supported the miners and ordered a general strike.

Key terms

Triple Alliance: an agreement made by the three biggest trade unions to support one another if one of them was engaged in an industrial dispute. It had been formed before the First World War and was renewed in 1920.

> 66 *Constitutional Government is being attacked. Stand behind the Government who are confident that you will co-operate in the measures they have taken to preserve the liberties of the people. The General Strike is a challenge to Parliament and is the road to ruin.* 99
>
> Stanley Baldwin, published in the British Gazette, 6 May 1926

B A message from the Prime Minister

> 66 *The TUC does not challenge the constitution. It does not want to undermine our Parliamentary institutions. Its sole aim is to secure for the miners a decent standard of life. It is engaged in an industrial dispute. There is no constitutional crisis.* 99
>
> From the British Worker, 7 May 1926

C The Trade Unions' view of the General Strike

Tasks

1 How useful is Source **A** in explaining why a general strike failed in 1921?

2 How do Sources **B** and **C** differ in their views on the reasons for the General Strike? Why do they differ?

Events of the General Strike

The General Strike lasted from 4 to 12 May 1926. Three million workers came out on strike in support of the miners. Key workers, such as those in hospitals or sewage works, were instructed not to strike. The response to the strike differed from area to area. In some areas there was little activity or violence. There were parades and meetings, and relations with the police were good. For many it was like a holiday. In other areas there were violent clashes between strikers and non-strikers that resulted in police action. There was damage to property – buses and trams were overturned, police stations were attacked.

In the period of the General Strike, three million workers went on strike. About 3,000 strikers were prosecuted for violent behaviour.

D *Waterloo Station, London, during the General Strike*

Sir Herbert Samuel, Chairman of the Samuel Commission, approached the TUC and offered to help bring the strike to an end. The TUC met Samuel and worked out a set of proposals to end the General Strike.

On 11 May, at a meeting of the TUC General Committee, it was decided to accept the terms proposed by Samuel and to call off the General Strike on 12 May.

Did you know ??????

Winston Churchill, Chancellor of the Exchequer during the General Strike, was also editor of the *British Gazette*. His reputation with the trade unions and the miners had been poor since 1910 when, as Home Secretary, he had sent troops into South Wales to break up a miners' strike.

 An armoured food convoy leaving the London Docks

Task

3 Look at Sources **D** and **E**. How useful are they in informing you about the General Strike?

Why the General Strike failed

There were a number of reasons why the General Strike failed. The government was well-organised for the strike. The Organisation for the Maintenance of Supplies (OMS) ensured that essential supplies were maintained. The armed forces were used. The government also won the propaganda battle in winning over the people. It had the support of most newspapers and produced its own paper – the *British Gazette*. This was important because one of the first groups of workers called out by the TUC when the General Strike began was the printers. Most newspapers appeared only in very brief form, if at all. The government also used the BBC for radio broadcasts opposing the strike.

The TUC was less well-organised. It had not planned for a general strike. Not all workers went out on strike, including many on the instructions of the TUC. Many trade unionists were worried that the dispute was becoming political. Although the TUC produced its own newspaper, the *British Worker*, the government's control of the media was far stronger.

Task

4 How reliable is Source **F** in describing the progress of the General Strike?

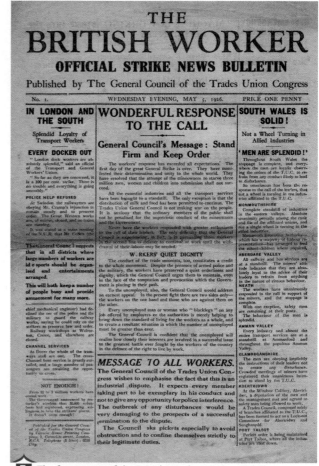

F *The front page of the* British Worker, *5 May 1926*

Opposition to the General Strike

The General Strike was not popular with the British people as a whole. The middle classes in particular opposed the Strike. They joined the OMS and volunteered to drive buses and trains, unload ships and became special constables. The churches opposed the Strike. Political parties opposed the Strike – even the Labour Party.

Pedestrian. "I'M AFRAID YOU'RE FULLY LOADED, AREN'T YOU?"
Owner-Driver. "NOT AT ALL, MADAM. THERE'S STILL ONE KNEE VACANT AT THE BACK, IF YOU DON'T MIND LETTING YOUR LEGS DANGLE OUTSIDE."

G A cartoon from a newspaper at the time of the General Strike

In June 1926, the government tried to get the miners and mine owners to reach an agreement. However, the mine owners announced new terms of employment for miners based on an 8-hour day. The miners refused to accept this and, although the General Strike was over, they continued their strike. For six months the miners held out, unsupported by the TUC. By November 1926, hardship and starvation forced them back to work. Finally, the miners were forced to accept longer hours and lower wages imposed by the mine owners.

The results of the General Strike were a disaster for the trade union movement. Membership fell. In 1927 the government passed the Trade Disputes Act which made a general strike illegal.

Task

5 How reliable is Source **G** in explaining public attitudes to the General Strike?

The reasons for the Depression in Britain

In the 1930s Britain was hit by economic **depression**. The old industries such as coal mining, textiles, shipbuilding, and iron and steel production were in decline. Methods of production were dated and inefficient. Britain began to lose export markets to newer industrial countries whose goods were of higher quality and were cheaper. The **Wall Street Crash** of 1929 in the USA made things worse. The USA recalled its loans and reduced its imports from Britain. As a result British industries began to close down and unemployment grew.

'Depressed Britain' in the 1930s

The old industries in decline tended to be based in the north of England, Wales and Scotland. In these areas the Depression hit hard. Where unemployment was high the whole community suffered. Shops and services closed down because people used them less. This further increased unemployment. Unemployed workers received the '**dole**' but this was subject to a means test where anyone claiming benefit had to prove that they needed it.

> ### Key terms
>
> **Depression**: a downturn in the economy of a country. Its common features are a fall in trade, the closure of factories and businesses, and high levels of unemployment. A cycle of depression is formed so that these features keep repeating themselves.
>
> **Wall Street Crash**: in 1929, the value of shares at the New York Stock Exchange on Wall Street plummeted. It caused the collapse of the world's most powerful economy and impacted on other countries' economies worldwide.
>
> **Dole**: the popular name for the benefit claimed from the state by the unemployed. All workers contribute to National Insurance while in work and the unemployment benefit comes from this fund.

H Map of the areas of heavy unemployment in the 1930s

Key
 Areas of heavy unemployment

Jarrow

Liverpool

Birmingham

Merthyr

London

I An unemployed man in Wigan

The effects of the Depression

> " Two thousand people assembled in pouring rain today outside the Broadway theatre, Manchester, to apply for 35 jobs. Two men walked from Oldham, 12 miles away. Half a dozen men had waited all night. The rain drenched those without overcoats and ran in streams from umbrellas, but no one would give up his or her position. "
>
> *From the* Manchester Evening News, 1932

J *The Depression in Manchester*

> " The popular image of the 1930s is of 'wasted years' – years of mass unemployment, dole queues, the means test and hunger marches. This is an image securely based upon reality for the many thousands of families who suffered the miseries of unemployment. "
>
> *From* The Slump, *J. Stevenson and C. Cook, 1979*

K *Two historians' view of the 1930s*

Task

6 How useful are Sources **H** to **K** in explaining the effects of the Depression?

The 'Jarrow Crusade' is a good example of the problems caused by the Depression. Jarrow is a town in the North East near Newcastle. The main employer in Jarrow was Palmers shipbuilding – the company employed up to 80 per cent of the town's working population. Others worked at the local colliery or the steel works. In 1930 the Jarrow colliery closed. In 1931 the steel works closed. Then in 1934 the shipyard shut down. Most of the town's workers were unemployed. In 1936 workers from Jarrow marched to London, a distance of nearly 300 miles, to ask the government to find them work. The Crusade took almost a month and received great support in the towns it passed through and much publicity – but few jobs resulted.

The north of Britain and South Wales were especially badly affected by the Depression. These areas were where most of Britain's traditional heavy industries such as coal mining, shipbuilding, steel and textiles were based. The decline in these industries brought great hardship to the people there.

Did you know ??????

When the Jarrow marchers arrived in London all that they were given was £1 each to get the train back to the North East.

> " There is no escape anywhere in Jarrow from its prevailing misery, for it is entirely a working-class town ... One out of every two shops appeared to be permanently closed. Wherever we went there were men hanging about, not scores of them but hundreds and thousands of them. "
>
> *From* The English Journey, *J.B. Priestley, 1934*

L *The writer J.B. Priestley describes a visit to Jarrow in 1933*

M The Jarrow Crusade on the march

'Prosperous Britain' in the 1930s

Not all of Britain suffered from the Depression of the 1930s. In London, the South East and the Midlands new industries were set up producing consumer goods such as motor cars, washing machines and radios. They used modern sources of power like electricity and modern methods of mass production. In these areas employment was high and wages were regular. Spending on consumer goods increased.

> *House building boomed. Many new private estates and urban developments appeared, especially in the South East. New industries appeared, again chiefly in the South East. For the majority of Britons the standard of living rose and, with developments like electricity, the radio and the spread of high street shops like* Marks and Spencer, *the quality of life improved too.*
>
> From Britain and Europe, 1848–1980, M. Roberts, 1987

N An historian explains the prosperity of the 1930s

Task

7 How useful are Sources **L** and **M** in explaining the effects of the Depression in Jarrow?

Did you know ??????

Cities like Birmingham, Coventry and Oxford prospered during the years of Depression because the motor industry was developing there. The number of cars on British roads doubled within the ten years of the 1930s.

Examples of prosperity

"B" TYPE HOUSE

Price:

FREEHOLD - - £815
LEASEHOLD - - £675

Including all Legal, Road, and Mortgage Charges.

TERMS OF PURCHASE:

Arrangements have been made for approved Purchasers to acquire
these houses on the following convenient terms:—

	Leasehold	Freehold
Deposit - -	£68 0 0	£82 0 0
Weekly Repayments	£ 0 18 9	£ 1 2 6
Ground Rent p.a.	£ 6 0 0	

SHOW HOUSE OPEN EVERY DAY INCLUDING SUNDAYS

O *New housing of the 1930s*

P *An advertisement from the 1930s for a vacuum cleaner*

Task

8 How useful are Sources **N**, **O** and **P** in informing you about the improved living standards in Britain in the 1930s?

Government actions to deal with the Depression

The Depression caused real problems for the government. Unemployment benefit had been paid to nearly all workers since 1922. However, the scheme was expected to pay for itself through contributions from workers and employers. As unemployment increased, so the contributions fell. More money was being paid out in benefits than the money coming in from those still in work.

This led to harsh actions by the government. Public expenditure cuts reduced the wages of all public servants – teachers were the worst hit with their pay reduced by 15 per cent. Even unemployment benefit was cut by 10 per cent. A **means test** was also introduced: the unemployed claiming benefit had to inform local officials what every person in the household was earning and what they had in savings. If elderly parent(s) lived in the family household even their old age pensions were counted as family income. So too did money a son earned from a paper round. This was then deducted from the amount of benefit received. The means test was unfair and degrading. People deeply resented this intrusion by 'outsiders'. Many unemployed workers refused to apply for unemployment benefit rather than give out personal details of their families.

Key terms

Means test: a system introduced by the government to make sure that the unemployment benefit paid out was fair. A person's and a family's sources of income were taken into account in deciding how much benefit a person should receive.

> 66 *The most cruel and evil effect of the means test is the way that it breaks up families. Old people are driven out of their homes. For instance, an old age pensioner, if a widower, would normally live with one of his children. His weekly pension goes towards the household expenses. Under the means test, however, he counts as a lodger and if he stays at home his children's dole will be docked.* 99
>
> From The Road to Wigan Pier, *George Orwell, 1937*

Q *The writer George Orwell comments on the means test*

The government also introduced measures to reduce the effects of the Depression. The Import Duties Act (1932) placed duties on goods from abroad of between 10 per cent and 20 per cent to make British goods more competitive and so encourage people to buy 'British'. This in turn would create jobs for British workers and reduce unemployment. The Special Areas Act (1934) provided government incentives of £2 million a year to attract new industries to old industrial areas like South Wales, southern Scotland, Tyneside and west Cumberland. Although useful, these measures had limited effect in creating jobs. The production of light industrial goods could not replace the jobs lost in labour intensive industries like coal mining and steel production. The approach of the Second World War was what really ended the Depression. The rearmament programme, extended in 1937, increased the demand for iron, steel, coal and ships.

Task

9 How reliable is Source **Q** in explaining the effects of the means test?

Did you know ??????

One Special Area on Tyneside was the Team Valley Industrial Estate in Gateshead, bringing light industry to the area. Although jobs were created, they could not replace those lost in the local coal mining and shipbuilding industries.

R *Unemployment 1929 to 1937*

Unemployed as a percentage of insured workers in regions of Great Britain			
	1929	**1932**	**1937**
London and SE England	5.6	18.7	6.4
SW England	8.1	17.1	7.8
Midlands	9.3	20.1	7.2
Northern England	13.5	27.1	13.8
Wales	19.3	36.5	22.3
Scotland	12.1	27.7	15.9
Northern Ireland	15.1	27.2	23.6

From Britain in the 20th Century World, *J. Traynor and E. Wilmot, 1994*

Tasks

10 Which four regions have the highest rate of unemployment from 1929 to 1937? Can you explain the reasons for this?

11 Which three regions have the lowest rate of unemployment from 1929 to 1937? Can you explain the reasons for this?

12 Is there evidence in the source to suggest that the Depression was coming to an end by 1937? Give a reason for your answer.

The Welfare State

A Labour government was elected in 1945 by a British people that wanted to see a real improvement in their living standards after the problems of the 1930s and the destruction of the Second World War. Building on earlier **Liberal reforms** (1906–14) and using the Beveridge Report (1942) as a basis, the government introduced a number of important reforms that would improve the welfare of the people.

The creation of the **National Health Service** (1948) was the most significant reform. This provided free medical, dental, hospital and eye treatment for all. Free medicine, spectacles and false teeth were also made available for all. Aneurin Bevan was Minister of Health when the National Health Service was created, and played the key role in introducing it.

Not everybody supported the introduction of the NHS. Many doctors were worried about losing their independence and some of their income if they went into the NHS. However, nearly all GPs had joined by the end of 1948.

> 66 *Dad had a small wage, and thought with a family of four children to bring up, it was too much money for him to be able to go to the doctor. He used to buy something from the chemist at sixpence a bottle that eased the pains in his stomach. But when he went to the NHS, this was thoroughly investigated and they found out that Dad had cancer. If he had been treated earlier, he could have been cured but, due to the expensive doctors, Dad died.* 99
>
> Quoted in Now the War is Over, P. Addison, 1985

A Health provision before and after the setting up of the NHS

Did you know ??????

The Beveridge Report (1942) came from a committee chaired by Lord Beveridge to suggest ways in which life in Britain could be improved after the war. It concluded that the state should support people 'from the cradle to the grave'.

> 66 *In the first year over 41 million people (95% of the population) were covered by the NHS. Over 8 million dental patients were treated and over 5 million pairs of spectacles given out. 187 million prescriptions were written out by more than 18,000 GPs. The NHS employed 34,000 people and cost nearly £400 million.* 99
>
> From 'Bevan's fight with the BMA', P. Jenkins, 1964

B The impact of introducing a National Health Service

Task

1 What evidence do Sources **A** and **B** produce to show that the NHS was needed?

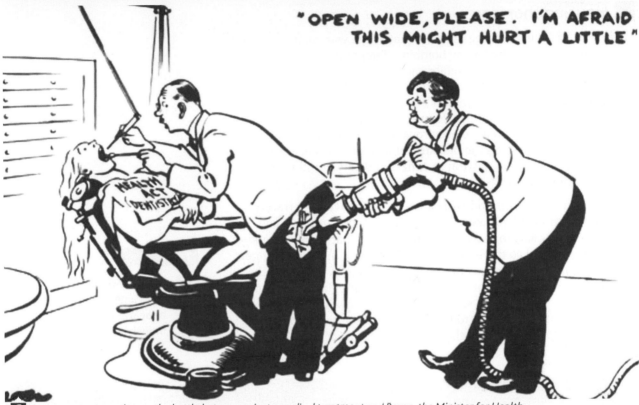

C   *A cartoon commenting on the battle between private medical treatment and Bevan, the Minister for Health*

As part of the reforms introduced by the Labour government, employers and employees paid national insurance contributions. These would go towards paying for new benefits as well as for the National Health Service.

National insurance was extended to provide benefits to:

- the old, building on the scheme introduced in 1908 by the Liberal government
- those off work through illness or out of work through unemployment, building on the scheme introduced in 1911
- the widowed and pregnant
- families through a Family Allowance
- those who needed additional support in the form of National Assistance.

None of these benefits was means tested – they came as a right.

People in work, except married women who were covered by their husbands' contributions, paid 4s 11d (about 25p) a week in national insurance contributions. This was about 5 per cent of an average weekly wage. James Griffiths, the Minister for National Insurance, claimed that it was 'the best and cheapest insurance policy offered to the British people, of any people anywhere.'

Task

2   Does this cartoon support or oppose the NHS? Give reasons for your answer.

Housing shortage

There was a serious shortage of housing after the war, mainly because of the damage caused by enemy bombing. Temporary accommodation was provided with 'prefabs' (prefabricated houses). Council housing estates were built to provide good houses for people to rent from the local authority. The New Towns Act (1946) provided money to set up new towns of about 50,000 people in each. These were built away from the large cities to reduce overcrowding. Twelve new towns were planned, most of them on the outskirts of London, such as Harlow, Basildon and Stevenage. Newton Aycliffe and Peterlee in the North East provided other new towns.

The old industrial towns had large areas of overcrowded, terraced housing with no gardens and with few green spaces around them. They were built close to the local factory gate so that workers could walk to work – and so the houses had the 'smell' of industry. The new towns were different. Houses were bigger and usually semi-detached. They had gardens at the front and back. They were planned around local amenities like shops, a school, a library, a park. The new houses allowed thousands of people to live in a much healthier environment than they had experienced in the old industrial towns.

Task

3 Look at Source **D**. How does a new town differ in appearance from an old industrial town?

D *An aerial view of the new town of Harlow*

Education

Before the war, there was no primary or secondary divide in education for the vast majority of children. They were educated from the ages of 5 to 14 in 'elementary' schools, after which they left school. Students could go on to a secondary grammar school but there were fees to be paid – unless a student was very able and won a 'scholarship'. Then the local authority paid the fees.

The Education Act of 1944, passed during the war, brought changes to this system. The Labour government now put the Act into operation. It divided education into primary and secondary, and introduced free secondary education for all. It also raised the school leaving age from 14 to 15. It also set up a 'tripartite' division of equal secondary schools. Three types of school were to be available to match a pupil's ability: secondary modern, technical and grammar.

The three types of schools were intended to be of equal standing, with parents deciding what was best for their child. However, it soon was obvious that too many parents thought that their children were 'academic' and chose the grammar school. So the '11+' examination was introduced and, based on the results of that, a child would be allocated to the type of school that matched his or her ability.

> **Did you know** ? ? ? ? ? ?
>
> The 11+ was an examination that tested a student's general ability to solve problems using maths and English – what we would call numeracy and literacy today.

> 66 *The majority of children learn most easily by dealing with concrete things and following a course rooted in their day to day experience. It is for this majority that the secondary modern school will cater.*
>
> *Some children, on the other hand, will have decided at quite an early stage to make their careers in branches of industry or agriculture requiring a special kind of aptitude in science or mathematics, music or art. All these pupils will find their best outlet in the secondary technical school.*
>
> *Finally, there will be a proportion whose ability and aptitude require the kind of course with the emphasis on books and ideas that is provided at secondary grammar school.* 99
>
> *Ministry of Education pamphlet No. 12, 1947*

E *The tripartite system of secondary education*

> 66 *Dad promised me a bike if I passed the 11+. I can't remember the day of the exam – I was too nervous. A few weeks later our class teacher read out the names of pupils who had to see the headmistress. Five of us out of a class of 35 went and were told that we had passed the 11+ and would be going to the grammar school. Some of my friends didn't pass. They wouldn't be my friends for much longer. While they were out playing football I was doing Latin and Physics homework.* 99

F *The author remembers how he felt when he passed the '11 plus' exam*

> **Task**
>
> 4 Look at Sources **E** and **F**. List the three types of secondary school and say what kind of pupil would attend each. Do you think that the types of schools were equal? Give reasons for your answer.

Nationalisation

Most industries had been under state control during the war. This 'nationalisation' now continued. The Labour government felt that the interests of the workers would be better protected. Profits made by the industries would go to the state to support the welfare reforms rather than to private owners. It also meant that the government would provide money to modernise these industries. In this way the problems that industry and workers had experienced between the wars would be removed. There was little opposition to the coal and railway industries being nationalised as both were expensive to operate and were unprofitable. There was much greater opposition to the nationalisation of iron and steel production as it was running at a profit at the time.

G *The nationalisation programme, 1946 to 1951*

1946	Bank of England		Air transport		
1947	Coal	Gas	Electricity	Railways	Road haulage
1951	Iron and steel				

The decline of empire in India and Africa

In 1900 Britain controlled a massive empire throughout the world on which 'the sun never set'. In the 20th century there had been some challenges to it, mainly from Ireland and India, but in 1945 it was still largely intact. The impact of the Second World War was about to change this.

The **nationalist** movement in India, led by Gandhi, had been strong before the war. During the war the 'Quit India' campaign developed with the aim of ending British rule of India. The British authorities in India tried to suppress this movement. Then in 1946 the new Labour government promised to give India its independence. This caused problems as 75 per cent of the population of British India was Hindu and 25 per cent was Muslim. The Muslims demanded a separate country. It was finally decided to partition British India into India (Hindu) and Pakistan (Muslim). Independence came in 1947. It brought with it much disruption as over 10 million Hindus and Muslims crossed the new boundaries, and resulted in much violence with over half a million deaths.

> ❝ *What are the alternatives we face in India? First, we could attempt to strengthen British control in India. This would mean a considerable increase in British troops there. Such a policy would mean a decision that we should remain in India for at least another 15 to 20 years.*
>
> *The second alternative is to persuade the Indians to come together. At the same time we would warn them that there is a limit of time during which we are prepared to maintain our responsibility in India.* ❞
>
> Sir Stafford Cripps, the main negotiator of the British government in India

H *The problems facing the government in Britain's rule of India*

THE ROPE TRICK

I *A cartoon showing Britain's problems in its rule of India*

Task

5 How accurate are Sources **H** to **J** in explaining the problems Britain faced in India in the late 1940s?

Timeline

Mahatma Gandhi

1869	born in India
1888–92	studied in London and graduated as a barrister
1893–1914	lived in South Africa and led a civil rights campaign to end discrimination of Indians there
1915	returned to India
1921–41	led the nationalist movement against British rule of India; used passive resistance as his main 'weapon'
1942	began the 'Quit India' campaign calling on Britain to leave India
1947	British rule in India ended; India divided into India and Pakistan
1948	assassinated by a Hindu who blamed Gandhi for the partition of India

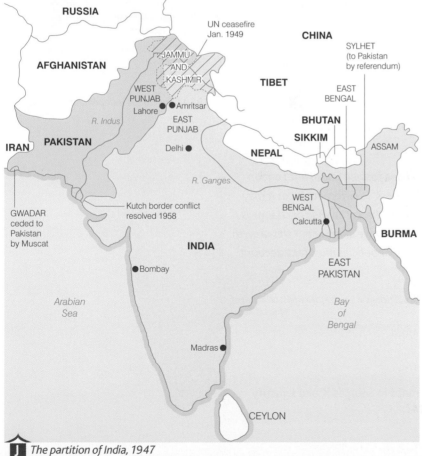

J *The partition of India, 1947*

Did you know ??????

Gandhi's birthday, 2 October, is a national holiday in India. In 2007 the United Nations adopted that day as an 'International Day of Non-Violence'.

The British in Africa

Britain had a large number of colonies in Africa. As in India, the Second World War weakened British control of these colonies and encouraged nationalist movements that demanded independence. Most movements were prepared to resort to violence against the British: for example, the Mau Mau rebellion in Kenya from 1952 to 1956. In 1960 the British Prime Minister, Harold MacMillan, recognised this in a speech in South Africa. By 1980 the British Empire's rule in Africa had come to an end.

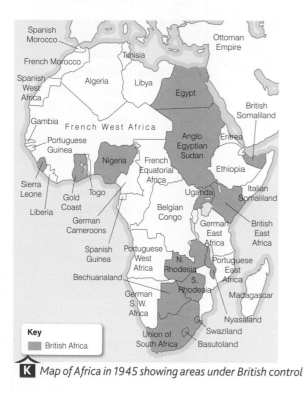

K Map of Africa in 1945 showing areas under British control

L Map of Africa in 1980 showing the independent states of Africa

> **❝** *The most striking of all impressions I have formed since I left London is the strength of African national consciousness. In different places it may take different forms, but it is happening everywhere. The wind of change is blowing through the African continent. Whether we like it or not this growth of national consciousness is a political fact. Our policies must take account of it.* **❞**
>
> *From a well known speech made by MacMillan to politicians in South Africa whilst on a tour of Africa in 1960*

M Harold MacMillan speaks of the change in Africa

Task

6 How far does a comparison of the maps in Sources **K** and **L** justify MacMillan's comments in Source **M**?

AQA Controlled Assessment style questions

1 **Source A** *Ben Turner, a trade union leader, speaking at a TUC conference in 1926*

'I want to express my great satisfaction with the General Strike. I think it was a great moment and a great effort. It will stand in our history as one of the great events that the trade union movement has indulged in.'

How far do Sources B to G in section 3.1 support this interpretation of the General Strike? You should also use your knowledge of the event to support your answer.

2 Study Sources H to M in section 3.1.

Explain how useful these sources are to you in examining the Depression of the 1930s in Britain.

3 **Source B** *The historian A.J.P. Taylor writing in 1965*

'Most people in Britain were enjoying a richer life in the 1930s than any previously known.'

How far do Sources I to Q in section 3.1 support this interpretation of British society in the 1930s? You should also use your knowledge of the period to support your answer.

4 Study Sources A to G in section 3.2.

Explain how useful these sources are in showing you how Britain had changed in the period after the Second World War.

5 'The British Empire ended because of the emergence of nationalist movements in its colonies.'

How far do Sources H to M in section 3.2 support this interpretation of the reasons for the end of the British Empire? You should also use your knowledge of the subject to support your answer.

4.1

The position and status of women in Britain in the early 1900s

A *Women working in a sewing factory at the start of the 20th century*

Women at the beginning of the 20th century

The position and status of women at the beginning of the 20th century was much better than it had been 50 years earlier, but women still did not have equal status with men, and this had not been fully achieved by the end of the 20th century. However, there were some improvements in the last 50 years of the 19th century which should not be forgotten and did show the way forward in 1900.

Daily life for women varied depending on social class. For working-class women there was work in the factories and for many poorer women a life as a domestic servant beckoned. Many poor girls from the country could only expect a life of cooking, cleaning and drudgery. Middle-class families could afford a number of servants, which freed women (and men) totally from the duties of housework and even from bringing up their own children. For these women a life of socialising and charity work lay ahead. Some middle-class women did gain entry to university. Many, however, turned to the growing issue of votes for women.

The changes in law for women

The legal position for women by the start of the 20th century had improved on the situation they found themselves in 50 years earlier. It was only in 1857 that women could divorce their husbands, and at this stage it was only on the grounds of cruelty. It was only after 1870 that they were allowed, in law, to keep money that they had earned themselves. Twenty years later a law was passed (1891) allowing women to leave their husbands, while in New Zealand women got the vote for the first time in 1893. Within 12 months a petition was signed by 250,000 people demanding that women in Britain were also given this right to vote in national general elections.

> **66** *Let women be what God intended, a helpmate for man, but with totally different duties and vocations.* **99**
>
> *From a letter written in 1870*

B *The views of Queen Victoria*

In 1900 a general election took place. Only 7 million men could vote out of a population of over 42 million. The new government, the Conservatives, was against giving women the vote. The other main parties, the Liberals and the Irish Nationalists, did not really want to see women voters either. The political parties were worried that in giving women the vote it might change the election results in favour of one of the other parties. It is important to remember that many ordinary working men did not have the vote either.

Women had been able to vote in council elections since 1869. People soon became used to women voting for councils, school boards and for boards of health. In a London County Council election of 1907 Lady Margaret Sandhurst was elected to the council. However, her opponent objected and the case went to court, only for Lady Sandhurst to be told she could not become a council member. The Acts of Parliament had only referred to women being able to vote in elections. Nowhere did they actually say that women could be elected themselves!

Did you know ??????

Who could actually vote in 1900?

About ²/₃ of the males in Britain could vote in 1900. These included: the upper classes, middle classes and some from the working class (males over 30 who owned or rented a house).

Did you know ??????

Lady Sandhurst's opponent was the son of Beresford Hope, a leading opponent of votes for women. He opposed her on the grounds that she was a woman. The election overseer actually disagreed with her opponent. The case was taken to court and the judge overruled.

Tasks

1. How useful is Source **A** in explaining the role of women at the start of the 20th century?

2. How useful is Source **B** in explaining the views of women at the start of the 20th century?

The role of the middle-class woman

> 66 My mother was a vicar's daughter and my father was a vicar's son and they went to church twice on Sunday. They were very good citizens: they read their Bible. My mother kept a beautiful larder full of jams and pickles. She saw that everything was cleaned. She did an enormous amount of very beautiful embroidery, and visited people on certain days. I just got bored with it. I would have done anything to escape this sort of life. 99

C From Alice Remington's memories of her life at home as a 15 year old in 1914. She lived in a middle-class family

> 66 That woman seems to think that the female clerk should receive the same wage as the male clerk for similar work. This is ridiculous. They are so fond of comparing their work as equal to the male clerk. I would suggest that they should fill their spare time washing out the office and dusting. You will agree this is more suited to their sex and would give them a little practice in the work they will be called upon to do if they actually decide to marry one of the poor male clerks whose jobs they are trying to take over. 99

From a letter written to the Liverpool Echo in 1911 after a woman had written to the newspaper demanding the same wages as a male clerk

D Working in a Liverpool office, 1911

Did you know ??????

Mrs Fawcett argued that since women had to pay taxes just as men did, they should have the same rights as men. Wealthy mistresses of large manors and estates employed gardeners, workmen and labourers who could vote, but the women could not, regardless of their wealth.

Tasks

3 How useful is Source **C** in explaining the role of middle-class women in 1900?

4 How reliable is Source **D**?

The education system

The education system played its part in preparing girls for their role in society. While all pupils studied the '3 Rs' (reading, writing and arithmetic) the other subjects showed what society expected. Boys would study woodwork, while girls learnt how to sew, clean, cook and even how to do the laundry. Girls were being prepared for a life in domestic service. Occasionally, bright girls could go further by gaining a scholarship. Ellen Wilkinson, who later became a Member of Parliament, went to Manchester Day Training College and later studied at Manchester University. University education was not unknown. Seventy young women gained places at university paid for by scholarships in 1910.

E An NUWSS rally being spoken to by their leader, Mrs Fawcett

Right to vote

Suffragists and Suffragettes, 1900–14

Women had not gained the right to vote by 1900. However, just as laws were changed in the fight for equality in the last years of the 19th century, women also began their campaign for the right to vote. The Primrose League and the Women's Liberation Foundation were two campaigning groups. The most famous of all, the National Union of Women's **Suffrage** Societies (NUWSS), was formed in 1897. With an eventual membership of over 50,000, it brought together over 500 local societies. It worked through legal means to try to secure the vote for women and, as a result, private members' bills were brought to the House of Commons. None of them was successful. However, it continued with its peaceful protest, ensuring it remained within the law.

> **Key terms**
>
> **Suffrage:** the right to vote in public elections.

F *Women peacefully protest against the Liberal party*

> **Did you know** ??????
>
> Though most men were opposed to votes for women, some leading male politicians supported universal suffrage. In 1907 the Men's League for Women's Suffrage was formed.

> **Task**
>
> **5** What do Sources **E** and **F** tell you about the NUWSS?

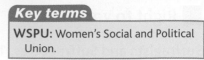

The methods of the NUWSS

Methods used by the NUWSS included:

- organising local groups of supporters
- holding public meetings with important speakers
- writing and distributing pamphlets
- collecting petitions
- talking to Members of Parliament
- getting Members of Parliament to put forward bills before the House of Commons (little chance of success).

Many women felt the NUWSS had failed. They believed that peaceful methods did not work. Although some private members' bills attracted support in the early 1900s, it became clear that the government (Conservatives and then from 1905 onwards Liberals) would not support the idea of votes for women. Some women thought that the campaign to get women the right to vote had to be pushed more aggressively.

The **WSPU** was founded in Manchester on 10 October 1903 by six women, including Emmeline and Christabel Pankhurst. Christabel soon became the leader. To begin with, their intention was to recruit more working-class women to their cause. However, in 1905 they decided to use more forceful methods to gain the public's attention.

On 13 October 1905 two members of the WSPU, Christabel Pankhurst and Annie Kenney, were arrested after disturbing a public meeting in Manchester. They were charged and fined. They refused to pay their fines and ended up in prison. This was front page news. The violent campaign had begun.

Did you know ??????

Christabel Pankhurst and Annie Kenney were at the meeting in Manchester to hear Sir Edward Grey, a minister in the British government. The two women shouted repeatedly throughout his speech, 'Will the Liberal government give votes to women?' They refused to stop shouting or to leave and eventually the police tried to evict them from the meeting. During the ensuing struggle a policeman claimed the two women kicked and spat at him.

G *Emmeline and Christabel Pankhurst photographed for the WSPU wearing their prison uniforms. This photograph was taken at the Pankhursts' home after they had been released from prison*

Task

6   **a**   How useful is Source **G**?

    b   How reliable is Source **G**?

Early in 1906 the WSPU moved its headquarters to London which provided more opportunities for 'staging spectacular demonstrations'. One such occasion was held on 'Women's Sunday' in June 1908 and united Suffragettes from across the country in several different processions through central London to Hyde Park. They then began a campaign against the new Liberal government because it did not seem to want to give women the vote. The WSPU knew that a strong public campaign would put the government under pressure. Even the leader of the NUWSS knew that the peaceful tactics of the past had less effect.

> **66** *One of the women, Mrs Pankhurst, spat in the face of two police officers and also hit one of them. There was no intention at that time to arrest them. In the street they were told both by the police and their own friends that they ought to go away quietly. They did not, and a policeman was again assaulted. The police withdrew, to give the ladies a chance of getting away. Had they gone, the matter would have been closed so far as the police were concerned. But the women were not satisfied. They began to yell and shriek, with the result that a large crowd gathered. It was then that the police arrested both of them.*
>
> *If the evidence was to be believed, their behaviour was such as one would expect of women from the slums.* **99**
>
> *From a description of the trial of Mrs Pankhurst published in the* Manchester Guardian, *6 October 1906*

H *A newspaper description of an assault on police officers by Mrs E. Pankhurst in 1906*

> **66** *I hope that the more old-fashioned suffragists [NUWSS] will stand by their friends who in my opinion have done more to bring the movement within the region of practical politics [the vote] in twelve months than I and my followers have been able to do in the same number of years.* **99**

I *Millicent Fawcett, leader of the NUWSS, writing to* The Times, *1906*

> **66** *The WSPU put back the chances of women gaining the vote by their violent campaign. It did little more than confirm many men's views that women did not deserve the vote.* **99**

J *A modern historian writing in 2009*

Tasks

7 How reliable is Source **H** in describing the incident involving Emmeline Pankhurst in Manchester in October 1906?

8 How do Sources **I** and **J** differ in their views on the violent campaign of the WSPU? Why do they differ? Use the content of each source and its provenance to explain your answer.

The methods of the WSPU

The more violent the WSPU became, the greater its publicity. For many women it seemed the way forward. Others felt it damaged any real chances for women to get the vote. However, the government reactions to the violent campaign actually brought the **Suffragettes** some new support as people did not like the ways in which the Suffragettes were treated by the authorities.

Methods used by the WSPU included:

- chaining themselves to railings in Downing Street
- attacking MPs who did not support them
- leafleting London from a hot-air balloon
- setting fire to postboxes
- damaging golf courses
- smashing windows on Oxford Street
- rioting at public meetings.

However, the most sensational event took place with the disruption of the Epsom Derby on 4 June 1913 when Emily Wilding Davison was fatally injured. It was believed she tried to stop the King's horse, Anmer, from possibly winning the Derby by running out in front of it. She died four days after the Derby from injuries sustained on that day.

HE DERBY TRAGEDY : AT TATTENHAM CORNER

A SUFFRAGETTE'S MAD RUSH AND ITS CONSEQUENCES

K *Newspaper report on the Epsom Derby, 1913*

> 66 *The most determined martyr of them all, Miss Emily Davison, red-haired, green eyed, half-demented girl, denied the sacrifice of her life when she leapt from the upper floor of Holloway Prison after a hunger strike, was killed in the end on Derby Day 1913. She flung herself under the flying hooves of the King's horse as it led the field, thundering round Tattenham Corner.* 99

An extract from a biography of Lloyd George

L *The death of Emily Wilding Davison, described by a biographer of Lloyd George, who, like Lloyd George, did not want women to gain the vote*

Task

9 How reliable are biographies like Source **L** to an historian?

> 66 *The horses were thundering down the course at a great pace bunched up against the rail. From the position in which the women were standing it would have been impossible for her to have picked out any special horse. It was obviously her intention to stop the race. Misjudging the pace of the horses she missed the first four or five. They dashed by just as she was emerging from the rails. With great calmness she walked in front of the next group of horses. The first missed her, but the second, Anmer, came right into her, and catching her with his shoulders, knocked her with terrific force to the ground while the crowd stood spellbound. Fortunately, Anmer fell clear of the woman, and the horses following swerved by the woman, the jockey and the fallen horse.* 99

M *An eyewitness account of the incident at Tattenham Corner, Epsom Derby 1913*

Did you know ??????

Frederick Lawrence was the son of Liberal parents. He was a lawyer and worked with the poor. He married Emmeline Pethick, a social worker, in 1901 and immediately added his wife's name to his own. The WSPU did not allow men to become members but Frederick used his legal training to represent the WSPU in court.

Task

10 Which source (**K**, **L**, **M**,) is the most reliable description of the Epsom Derby, 1913?

The Cat and Mouse Act

The events of 1912 and 1913 had a huge effect on the suffrage movement. The WSPU began to split. Many members could not accept the growing violent campaign and they left. The NUWSS decided to have nothing to do with them and key supporters like Emmeline and Frederick Pethick-Lawrence left.

The government tried to find ways of dealing with the Suffragettes in prison and passed the Prisoners (Temporary Discharge) Bill. This soon became known as the Cat and Mouse Act, and by allowing Suffragettes to temporarily leave prison once they became ill when on hunger strike, then re-arresting them once they regained their health, it played into their hands. Propaganda photos and public appearances made the new law very ineffective. As the First World War approached, Parliament became even more determined not to give in to the Suffragettes' violent campaign.

Did you know ??????

Emmeline Pankhurst was jailed 11 times in succession in 1913–14.

The role of women in the First World War

When war broke out in August 1914, the WSPU decided to suspend its campaign in order to support the war effort. Generally, people thought the war would be over by Christmas. In the first nine months of the war little happened. Women were encouraged to knit for the troops and even Christabel Pankhurst attended recruiting rallies and encouraged young men to sign up. Things changed rapidly in 1915. As 2.5 million men signed up and a shortage of munitions showed, there was clearly a need for women to get more involved in the war effort.

Women at work in the First World War:

- Munitions factories
- Nursing
- Farm workers (Land Army)
- Motor car industry
- Aircraft industry
- Clerical work
- Banking
- Postal workers
- Bus conductresses

Women in the armed forces in the First World War:

- Women in the First Aid Nursing Yeomanry (FANY)
- Voluntary Aid Detachment (VAD)
- Women's Auxiliary Army Corps (WAAC)
- Women's Royal Navy Service (WRNS)
- Women's Royal Air Force (WRAF)

Did you know ??????

Women working in munitions factories were nicknamed 'canaries' because the TNT they dealt with turned their skin yellow.

⚬⚬links

See pages 23–24 for more information on the role of women in the First World War.

66 *It is quite impossible to keep pace with all the new incarnations of women in wartime – 'bus-conductress, ticket-collector, lift-girl, club waitress, post-woman, bank clerk, motor-driver, farm-labourer, guide, munitions maker. There is nothing new in the function of ministering angel: the nurses in hospital here or abroad are only carrying out, though in greater numbers than ever before, what has always been woman's mission. But whenever he sees one of these new citizens, or hears fresh stories of their address and ability, Mr Punch is proud and delighted.* 99

From Punch *magazine, June 1916*

N *Women in wartime, according to Mr Punch*

Task

11 Do you think 'Mr Punch' would give women the vote? Explain your answer.

O *Woman working in a munitions factory machining the casings for tank artillery*

P *Women working on rockets in a munitions factory*

Q *Women laying a road surface*

Task

12 How useful are the photographs in Sources **O**, **P** and **Q** in illustrating the role and importance of women during the First World War?

The political impact of women's roles in the First World War

The support from women during the First World War was not to be forgotten, but it is not as simple as saying war work got women the vote. Many men did not like women doing 'their jobs' and there were even strikes against women workers early in the war. At the end of the war, many women were forced to give up the jobs that had given them so much personal freedom and a good wage. Fashion for women had even changed with new hairstyles, clothes that were more practical (including wearing trousers!) and a growing belief that they really were the equal of any man.

As the war rumbled on, the government had to address the issue of voting rights. It had decided in 1916 that any new laws would give all men over 21 the right to vote. If men were to fight in the trenches together then it was felt they deserved the vote. Many also now believed that women also deserved the vote. Even Herbert Asquith, who had previously been against women voting, was now in favour, and most people believed that without the women's contribution to the war effort the war might have been lost. The Representation of the People Act, 1918, was a victory for men as well as women. Men got the vote at 21, with women getting the vote at 30 years of age. However, only 6 million women (out of 13 million) qualified for the vote. If all women over 21 had been given the vote then they would actually have outnumbered the men. In 1928 a second Representation of the People Act was passed, giving women the vote at 21, on the same terms as men. Emmeline Pankhurst died just a few days after the Act of Parliament became law.

Did you know ??????

Many MPs believed that reform was inevitable and that by allowing some women the vote in 1918, it would keep the suffragists happy but also delay more radical reform – such as full and equal voting rights for men and women.

Task

13 Select five sources from Sources **A** to **Q**, which you feel best illustrate the determination of women to be the equal of men in the period 1900–18. Carefully explain your choice.

4.2 | The position and status of women in Britain after 1939

■ The role of women in the Second World War

When the Second World War broke out, many men hoped that their wives would be able to stay at home while they fought against Nazi Germany. The Separation Allowance was less than most men had earned before the war, so many women began to look for new employment opportunities. At first jobs were scarce, and then as the war effort gathered pace the government began to look for ways in which to recruit women into essential work. Propaganda campaigns were used but these were less effective than expected. The posters were vague and did not make it clear what the jobs entailed or what the rate of pay might be. Many women said that they were too busy looking after their families!

Task

1 How useful is Source **A** in explaining the recruiting campaign at the start of the war?

In March 1941 a new law was established which meant that all women between the age of 19 and 40 had to register at an employment exchange. They could then be directed into specific jobs to support the war effort. In reality there were many exceptions to this rule. Women with children under 14 did not have to take up war work, but they could still volunteer. Married women had to be found jobs near home, while single women could be sent almost anywhere. Long hours meant that women were not always happy in what they did.

A *Second World War recruiting poster encouraging women to Come into the factories*

> 66 *I never seem to see my babies now. I miss it, dressing them and feeding them, and I sort of feel that they'll forget their Mummy. Starting at six in the morning and getting back at nine, all I see of them is when they're asleep.* 99
>
> *From a Government Report, 1943*

B *Working mothers*

Task

2 How reliable is Source **B**?

3 How far does Source **B** about working mothers reflect the position in families at the end of the 20th century?

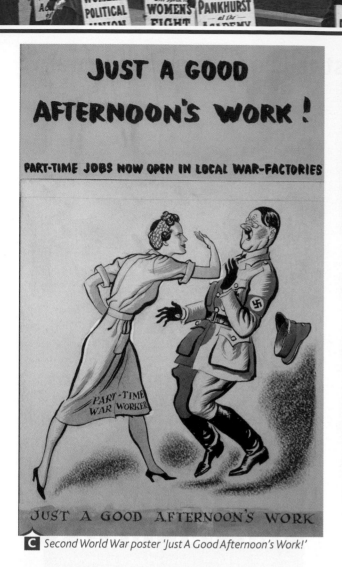

C Second World War poster 'Just A Good Afternoon's Work!'

D Welding for the war effort

Although most of the images of women in the Second World War were very positive and women generally seemed quite happy, they did have to put up with low pay, boring work and little chance of promotion. However, many learnt new skills as they became welders, engineers and even pilots.

Women at work in the Second World War:

- Post women
- Civil service
- Air-raid wardens
- Bus and tram conductresses
- Land Army
- Munitions factories

Women in the armed forces in the Second World War:

- The Auxiliary Territorial Service (ATS)
- The Women's Royal Navy Service (WRNS)
- The Women's Auxiliary Air Force (WAAF)

Did you know ??????

The government posters tried to make the work of the Women's Land Army look glamorous and exciting. In fact, the work was hard and young women usually worked in isolated communities, often living in old farm buildings with no electricity or running water.

Did you know ??????

In 1943 women at the Rolls Royce factory in Glasgow went on strike because skilled female workers were being paid less than unskilled men. The women won a partial victory and returned to work on the same pay as a male semi-skilled worker.

E   *Women members of the transport corps taking on the work of mechanics – notice their uniforms*

Task

4   How reliable are Sources **E** and **F** in illustrating the new role for women in the Second World War?

Women became increasingly involved in active roles in the Second World War. Some anti-aircraft guns were manned by men and women, and the women were quite capable of making the calculations necessary to aim the guns at enemy aircraft. They were just not allowed to fire them! Women acted as spies and members of the resistance movement fighting in France. Women flew Spitfires and Hurricanes from factories to RAF airfields.

A huge range of new job opportunities were presented to women during the war as they played their part in the war effort. As in the First World War, there were also some increased freedoms which were not without their own dangers.

The end of the war brought its own problems as husbands and wives tried their best to readjust to civilian life. Marriages made in the midst of war could be difficult to maintain as were the marriages or planned marriages of British women to American servicemen. Rationing continued well after the war ended and people, although relieved the war had ended, found themselves hoping for a better life.

Did you know **? ? ? ? ? ?**

Women secret agents were parachuted into occupied France as members of the Special Operations Executive. The most famous were Violette Szabo, who was murdered by the Gestapo, and Odette Churchill, who was captured and tortured. Both were awarded the George Cross.

Task

5   How useful is Source **F** to the study of women pilots in the Second World War?

F   *Women pilots of the Second World War; women were used to ferry planes from factories to the airfields*

Post-war legislation to promote equality for women

Women's experience of the Second World War had been very different from the First World War. They did in many cases do the same sort of work as they had done in the First World War. They worked on farms, as nurses and had put on military uniforms. However, in the 1939–45 war they had had to register for work and were in the front line. One thing had not changed. When the war ended they were expected to return to the jobs they had held before the war. By 1947 over 2 million women had left work and returned to the home.

By 1947 there was a labour shortage. Women had to be persuaded to go back to work. Many had missed the wages, even if they were traditionally lower than men's wages. They also missed the friendships that working provided.

As the 1940s and 1950s progressed, many women found the traditional role of mother, wife and homemaker more difficult to follow when they had experienced so much freedom in the war years. Equally, many marriages ended as returning soldiers could not fall back into the pattern of married life they had previously left behind.

Attitudes of young people had changed by the time the 1950s drew to a close. Greater freedom and more money in their pockets meant that young people experienced more independence than ever before. At the start of the 1960s young women seemed to demand a level of equality with men that had never been expected ever before. Television spread new ideas about equality and increasing numbers of women went to university. However, a '**glass ceiling**' still existed and by the end of the 1960s the fight for equality and for the end of sex discrimination was under way.

The year 1968 saw the 40th anniversary of the Act which gave at least some women the vote on equal terms with men. It seemed to stimulate the new campaign for equality. An Equal Pay Act had been passed in the USA in 1963. Many women in Britain wanted this too.

During 1969 women's liberation groups grew and made their demands for equality. Their work was successful, as in the following year the Equal Pay Act became law.

> **Key terms**
>
> **Glass ceiling:** an invisible upper limit. This term was used to describe the limited advancement of women in the workplace due to discrimination, as if there were an invisible ceiling which women could not pass through and so would not be able to rise to the top of the company.

> 66 *I wasn't prepared to just sit back and accept the role that my mother had. She was clever but had not had the chance to get a decent job because she'd spent all her time looking after kids. I wanted a good job, and it was good to be surrounded by women who felt the same.* 99

G *An interview with a woman who was 19 years old in 1968*

THIS OFFICER THIS UNIFORM AND AN EXECUTIVE JOB BEFORE SHE'S 23

This is the working dress of the Women's Royal Army Corps. It's couturier-designed, in a shade of lovat green and individually tailored.

She's got an executive job in her own right. Few girls under 23 can match this W.R.A.C. Officer's seniority and status—she makes decisions, issues instructions and takes responsibility. All the time she maintains her femininity. Just look at her stylish W.R.A.C. uniform! She will probably go abroad during her service, to Germany, the Mediterranean or the Far East. Pay and holidays are generous. There are as many kinds of officer appointments as there are intelligent girls. To apply for a commission you should be educated to sixth form standard and aged between 17 and 35. *Join the decision makers now!* Your first new decision may be the best you ever made—*to start a new kind of life in the W.R.A.C.* Fill in your name and address in the box below and post it off.

TO : LT. COL. BARBARA RIDLER, W.R.A.C., W.R.A.C. OFFICER ENTRY, LANSDOWNE HOUSE, BERKELEY SQ., LONDON, W.1. *Please send me further information about the W.R.A.C.*

Name   Date of Birth

H *A 1960s advert encouraging women to join the Women's Royal Army Corps*

Tasks

6 How far does Source **H** show increased equality for women in the 1960s?

7 How far does Source **H** depend on a stereotypical image of women to suggest growing equality?

Legislation in the 1970s

The Equal Pay Act, 1970:

- Equal pay for men and women
- Equal holidays, pensions, bonuses
- Equal work had to lead to equal pay
- If you could prove that the work you did was the same as a man's job, it was of equal value and you were entitled to equal pay

The Sex Discrimination Act, 1975:

- No discrimination in the workplace on the grounds of sex
- No discrimination on the grounds of marital status

In 1976 the Domestic Violence Act was also passed. It helped establish refuges for women and their children who needed to live somewhere secretly so that a violent husband or partner could not continue to assault them.

Position and status of women in Britain in 2000

The position of women in society is quite difficult to assess. You will always get different views. It depends who you talk to and what information you decide to use. The evidence you select might even tell you something about your own viewpoint. Even at the end of the 20th century, evidence suggests that 20 per cent of women face the sack once they tell their employer they are pregnant. Only one in ten directors in the British film industry is a woman, and even in government, Britain is only fourteenth in the European parliaments' league table for women representatives (out of a total of 25).

Many people believe that the glass ceiling is still something which most women cannot break through.

> 66 I'm a male working for a major multinational household brand, and have to say I think this is nonsense. Most of the high positions in management, as well as directorships, are held by women in our company. This doesn't bother me in the slightest, but I don't see any evidence of this so-called glass ceiling here. 99
>
> *Anon, Scotland*

> 66 I am a woman and I have a career, but no kids (yet). My opinion on the glass ceiling is that it exists, but perhaps women can't have it all ... I don't think that a woman can be a good mother AND a high flying career woman (well, not until the kids have grown up). 99
>
> *Jo, London*

> 66 I can only speak on behalf of my wife but I feel there is quite definitely career discrimination against women going off to have a family. My wife lectured at a college of further education and the availability of meaningful career opportunities changed radically when she told them she was pregnant. It was clear that this was all a major inconvenience and my wife is convinced to this day that had her job not been protected by law, she would have been obliged to leave. 99
>
> *Michael Gemson, Rolleston, UK*

I Views from a blog on women's rights at the end of the 20th century

Task

8 Use Source **I** to explain what people feel about the glass ceiling.

Equality?

It would be incorrect to think that the position of women at the end of the 20th century was not significantly better than at the beginning. In the space of 100 years much has changed and there are many examples of women in key positions in business and politics. It is, however, quite important to realise that the battles for equality are regularly being won but few women, or men, feel that the war is over.

J *The Spice Girls get back together*

K *Britain's first female Chief Constable, Pauline Clare, 1995–2002*

L *Deborah Meadon, successful businesswoman from the TV programme* Dragons' Den

Task

9 Do Sources **J** to **L** prove that women had gained equality by 2000? Explain your answer.

Activity

Equality for women at the end of the 20th century

1 You should research the position of women in 2000 by considering some of the following:

- Successful women in business – Deborah Meadon, Anita Roddick, J.K. Rowling
- Successful women in politics – Margaret Thatcher
- Successful women in the media – Madonna, The Spice Girls, Kate Silverton
- Successful women – personal or local study

AQA Controlled Assessment style questions

1   'Women were happy to work in factories and offices and accepted that their key role in life was as the manager of the home.'

Study Sources A to F in section 4.1. How far do these sources support this view of women before the First World War?

2   Study Sources K to M in section 4.1.

Explain how useful these sources are to you in examining the events at the Epsom Derby, 1913.

3   Select **three** sources (from Sources G to Q in section 4.1) which show that many women did not support the violent campaign of the Suffragettes. Explain how they support this view.

4   'Women played a greater role in the Second World War compared with their role in the First World War.'

Do you agree? Use **five** sources to illustrate whether you agree or disagree with this statement.

5   Study Source I in section 4.2. They are blog entries from a website.

Explain how useful these sources are to you in examining the views on the changing role and status of women.

6   'Women achieved equality with men by the end of the 20th century.'

Use sources and your own knowledge to say how far you agree or disagree with this statement.

Question 1

Select five sources. Explain how useful these sources have been in informing you in your enquiry into the war in the air in World War 1 and World War 2.

(15 marks)

Objectives

In this chapter you will learn about:

selecting a range of different types of sources to improve an answer to the Historical Enquiry questions

how to develop good level answers to the two Historical Enquiry questions

how the mark scheme operates in the two Historical Enquiry questions.

The following sources were selected for this enquiry.

A *World War 1 painting of a dogfight in the air*

B *A newspaper headline from the Battle of Britain*

> ❝ *Aeroplanes were still a new invention when the First World War broke out. Their first use was for reconnaissance, scouting the location of the enemy. Photographs taken from the air could pinpoint enemy positions. Aircraft could also be used for artillery observation; a plane equipped with a radio could identify whether an artillery gun was hitting its target and radio back directions if it wasn't.* ❞
>
> From an article by Nick Poyntz, Hindsight, April 2008

C The use of aeroplanes in World War 1

Bonn	83%
Hamburg	75%
Dusseldorf	64%
Cologne	61%
Dresden	59%
Munich	54%
Frankfurt	52%

D *Percentage of German cities destroyed by Allied air attacks in World War 2*

E A German plane flying over London during the Blitz, September 1940

A good range of different types of sources has been selected. In terms of the coverage of the topic, there is again a broad range with two sources on World War 1 and three on World War 2. They also look at different aspects of war in the air. The weakest source may be the photograph of the Blitz – it does not really tell you a great deal and it would need background knowledge to fully understand it.

Answer

Fighting in the air was just developing in World War 1 and the use of planes was limited by what they could do. Planes were used for photographing enemy positions, and the German Zeppelins used to bomb London. By World War 2 the technology of aeroplanes had improved. They were faster, better armed and better equipped. This meant that they could be used in more deadly ways like the bombing of towns. However, the general uses of aeroplanes in the two World Wars were not that different.

> **AQA Examiner's comment**
>
> In some ways this is a good introduction. It summarises how planes were used in the two World Wars and makes comparisons. There is a major weakness – the target of the question is to analyse and evaluate five sources but there is no mention of the sources here. A better introduction would be to comment on how the sources were selected and link them to the knowledge here.

The sources selected showed that in both World Wars there were dogfights between aeroplanes – fights in the air. The painting in Source A shows a dogfight between British and German planes in World War 1. The painting also shows how an extra seat was put in planes to allow a machine gunner to be placed at the back to protect the pilot. The painting gives a good indication of what aeroplanes in World War 1 looked like – clumsy and not made from strong materials. Dogfights like this became common as the war progressed either in one or two seater planes. Fighting aces became heroes. Baron von Richthofen was the most famous German ace. The painting is useful in showing a dogfight in World War 1. However, it is a painting and can only be a personal view of what a dogfight looked like.

Dogfights also took place in World War 2. The planes used, like the Spitfire and the Messerschmitt, were faster, better armed and less clumsy than in World War 1. The Battle of Britain saw many dogfights and Source B describes an air battle of 15 September 1940. It explains how enemy aircraft crossed the Channel to support the bombing raids on Britain. In this case London may have been the target because Buckingham Palace was bombed. The RAF sent up fighters to attack the enemy. The report states that 175 German planes were shot down. The number of planes involved shows a main difference from the dogfights of World War 1. The source is from a British newspaper so its usefulness has to be questioned. It will have been censored by the government. Also the government would have released the figures so there is no way of knowing whether they are accurate. The government would want to keep up morale by showing the British people that we are 'taking on' the Germans. Newspapers would be expected to play their part. This might explain the comment that the 'RAF puts Goering [Head of the Luftwaffe] in shade'. All I can say for certain is that there was an air battle and it involved a large number of planes.

> **AQA Examiner's comment**
>
> The answer starts well by not going through each source one by one. Instead themes based on war in the air are chosen. The first theme of aerial combat compares Sources A and B. For both sources there is good analysis to explain their meaning – source description is avoided. You can also see that there is good supporting knowledge. Source B has some good evaluation – its limitations are clearly discussed in terms of provenance. Source A is also evaluated but more generally – the comments on the usefulness of the painting are simple. In particular there is no comment on the provenance. Who painted it? Why was it painted?

The sources also show that there were differences in the war in the air in the two World Wars because of differences in technology. Source C gives a short description of how planes were used in World War 1. It explains how their use was limited to finding information to help the ground forces. It is very clear that the main method of fighting was on land not air. Planes would find where the enemy positions were – either by photography to advise ground troops or by radio to direct ground artillery. The source is a secondary source from a historical magazine. It can be accepted as reliable and useful in explaining how aeroplanes were used in the fighting in World War 1. However, it does not tell me everything that aeroplanes were involved in. For example there is no mention of the dogfights or the bombing raids on Britain by German Zeppelins.

By the time of World War 2 the development of aircraft meant that long range bombers could attack civilian targets. The aim was to weaken morale, using tactics like the Blitz on London, or to destroy key industrial targets. This made World War 2 much more of a total war than World War 1. This is seen in saturation bombing. Source E is a photograph of a German plane flying over London during the Blitz in September 1940 – the same time as the report in Source B. It shows how difficult it was to stop enemy planes flying over towns. If the RAF failed to stop them, only the AA defences were available and these were not that accurate in their fire. The source also shows the damage that could be caused by dropping bombs on built-up areas. However, the source is a photograph: it only shows us one enemy plane flying over London at one time so its usefulness is limited.

Source D also gives details about saturation bombing in World War 2, this time by British bombers. It shows the damage done to German cities. It is useful because it gives information on the scale of the bombing. It also suggests that the targets were not only industrial because, if the bombing had been selective, the amount of total damage to towns would not have been so great. However there are limitations to this source. It doesn't say how the figures were calculated. Bonn was bombed to a greater extent than Cologne or Frankfurt but it may not have been by that exact amount. The figures don't show when the bombings took place. For example one bombing raid on Dresden in February 1945 killed 25,000 civilians and destroyed much of the city centre. Does that account for the 59 per cent of damage caused to Dresden?

AQA Examiner's comment

The second theme of the answer is a difference in war in the air in the two World Wars. All three sources show good analysis – again source description is avoided. Knowledge is used to explain the content – more particularly in Sources D and E. Sources C and E are well evaluated – the strengths and limitations in their usefulness are explained in detail. Source E has more simple evaluation comments on the limitations of photographs in general – as in Source A above.

The five sources selected show that in the two World Wars there are similarities in the kind of fighting carried out in the air. There are also differences mainly caused by the technical development of aircraft – in particular the saturation bombing of World War 2 could not have happened in World War 1.

AQA Examiner's comment

This is not a strong conclusion. It repeats what has been said in the opening paragraph. It makes only general reference to the sources. A better conclusion would be to make some judgement on how useful the sources have been in the enquiry. Which sources were the most useful and why? Which sources were least useful and why? Was one type of source more useful than another?

Examiner's assessment of the answer

The word count for the answer is about 875 words – slightly more than the 800 words that are advised in the Specification although there would be no penalty for exceeding the advice. If the candidate wanted to reduce the word count then some of the knowledge could be removed – this accounts for only three of the 15 marks for this question.

The answer has many good points with a sound structure and development. It is clearly stronger than Level 2 because of the depth of source analysis and evaluation. The answer satisfies all the areas of Level 3 – source analysis, source evaluation and supporting knowledge. So is it worth Level 4?

- source evaluation is not consistently developed. It is good for three sources (B, C, D) but rather general on Sources A and E
- a judgement is not made on how useful the five sources have been.

This places the answer in Level 3, towards the upper end of it. The mark range for the level is 8–12 marks. An appropriate mark would be 11.

Question 2

'Women played a far greater role in the war effort in World War 2 than in World War 1.'

How far do the sources you have used support this interpretation of the role of women in the two World Wars?   *(25 marks)*

The following sources were selected for this enquiry.

A *World War 1 painting by Edward Skinner,* For King and Country

66 *Before the Second World War I'd worked in a fruit shop. Once the war broke out and men joined the army I was told to work in Cargo Fleet steel works in Middlesbrough. We helped make the steel that was needed for the war effort. Some of the work was very hard. There were always some men around who had not been called up. They gave the orders and told us what to do. When the war ended we (the women) left the steel works. We had no choice – but I was happy to go.* 99

B *Alice Hewitson, aged 88, from an interview in 2008*

C   A recruitment poster for the
Women's Land Army in World War 2

66 We got a pair of brown corduroy breeches and then we had hob nail boots, green jerseys and leggings. Then we got a Land Army hat and a mac. My wage was 18 shillings (90p) a week in the Land Army. We had to pay 12 shillings (60p) for board and that left us with 6 shillings (30p) to go and enjoy ourselves. We were all sent to different places and I was sent to a vegetable farm. It was nothing but potatoes, greens, onions and all the rest of it. Of course everything was old fashioned there – no tractors in those days. Everything had to be done by hand. 99

From War Women of Britain: Women at War 1914–1918, *J. Hunt and IWM, 1992*

D   Mrs Grace Elsey recalls being a member of the Women's Land Army in World War 1

66 Attitudes to women workers remained, in many instances, negative. The ability of women to take on what had been men's work meant that increasing numbers of males were vulnerable to conscription. Some women doing skilled work had the full cooperation of male employees. Many other women were restricted to less skilled work and were victims of hostility and even sabotage. 99

From War and Society in Britain, 1899–1948, *R. Pope, 1991*

E   Attitudes to women workers in World War 1

F   A recruitment poster for the armed
forces in World War 1

G   A recruitment poster for the WAAF
from World War 2

66 As Britain used every resource to ensure national survival, it was in line with past experience that women should play a great part in the war economy. Four-fifths of the total addition to the labour force between 1939 and 1943 consisted of women who had not previously been employed or who had been housewives – and this was done without massive protest. Britain was the only country in the war where the government took full powers to conscript and direct women – including to work in war industries. 99

From British Society, 1914–1945, *J. Stevenson, 1984*

H   The role of women in World War 2

A very good range of different types of sources has been selected. There is a good balance to the sources with four each on the two World Wars. More importantly there is a good balance of sources that agree and disagree with the interpretation in the question: five would broadly disagree with it and three broadly agree with it. The choice of sources means that:

- the answer should be balanced in its judgements
- there is a good range of sources to analyse and evaluate.

Answer

World War 1 and World War 2 were the first total wars. Everyone had a part to play in the wars, not just the armed forces. My enquiry looks at the role of women in the two World Wars. I have chosen sources to cover both wars, four on each war to get a balance. I also found sources that agree and disagree with the interpretation in the question. I looked for different types of sources that showed the role women played in the World Wars.

This is a short but sound introduction for two reasons:

- it provides some factual background of why the role of women was important in the two World Wars
- it makes reference to the sources chosen and links them to the question and the interpretation. In other words the student gives a clear impression that he/she knows what the task is about.

Some sources disagree with the interpretation. They show that women played a similar role in both wars because they took on jobs that in peacetime would have been done by men. One area of work was on the land. In World War 1 the Women's Land Army (WLA) was set up to replace farm labourers who had joined the forces with Land Girls. Source D is from someone who joined the WLA. It gives the idea of an 'army'. There was a kind of uniform. They were sent to different places. This shows that they were part of an organisation. The source was produced by the Imperial War Museum and this makes it reliable. However, it has limitations. I don't know who Mrs Elsey was, where she worked or when she made these comments. If it was a long time after World War 1 then her memory could have failed or she might remember only the things she wanted to. Also this is only one person's memory of the war.

Source C shows that the WLA in World War 2 had a similar role – to produce the food that Britain needed to prevent starvation caused by U-boat attacks on merchant shipping. There is another similarity. The dress of the woman in the poster is like the description in Source D. The source shows me that the government thought that the WLA was important to the war effort. However, the purpose of the source reduces its reliability. The government wanted to persuade women to join the WLA so it was trying to make the work look attractive – a 'healthy, happy job' done by a smiling young woman.

A case is made that women performed a similar role on the land in both wars. The content of the sources is analysed – not described. Both sources are evaluated for their utility and reliability, and their limitations are pointed out. There is also good supporting knowledge linked to the sources.

Women also made a similar contribution in both wars in munitions and heavy industry, replacing men who were away fighting. Source A is a painting of women working in a munitions factory in World War 1 making shells. It shows that women played a major role here – only one man can be seen. However, it has limitations. The artist was commissioned by the government to paint the picture. It was painted during the war so its purpose might be to boost morale and show that everyone was getting involved in the war effort and to encourage women to work in the munitions industry. So Skinner paints an attractive picture of the work. This wasn't the case. The hours were long and the work was dangerous with the use of chemicals that could explode or cause disease.

Source B is an oral piece of evidence from World War 2. It explains how Alice Hewitson had to work in the local steel works to produce steel for war equipment in the place of men who had been called up. It was skilled work and women had to be trained to do it. Thousands of women went to work in heavy industry including munitions. The limitations are that it is the statement of one person given over 60 years after the war. So her memory might have faded or she may only remember certain things.

Taking Sources A, B, C and D together, they show that the interpretation is wrong. Women played a similar role in the war effort in both World Wars. The sources cover only two types of employment but there were others – nursing for example, or replacing men as bus drivers.

> **AQA**
> **Examiner's comment**
>
> A further case is made that women performed a similar role in both wars although there is not an exact comparison as for land. Again both sources are analysed to explain their meaning and both are evaluated. The supporting knowledge is good. The final summary paragraph in this section is good. It links the sources with the interpretation. It also provides knowledge to further support the case against the interpretation. The reference to nursing and other jobs is relevant and is the right length. There may have been a temptation to extend the knowledge here – but it is not directly related to the sources and would draw the answer away from the source evaluation required by the question.

The position of men working on the Home Front was still greater than that of women in both World Wars. Source E, covering World War 1, explains why. It was partly fear of losing their jobs and partly fear that they could be conscripted to the army. The source was written by an historian in 1991. It can be accepted as reliable and accurate although no examples of the mistreatment of women are given. Source B shows that men were in charge in World War 2 and tells me that, once the war was over, men returned to their previous jobs. So in both World Wars women were not given an equal role with men.

> **AQA**
> **Examiner's comment**
>
> This is a different kind of similarity in the roles of women in the two wars. The paragraph focuses on source analysis with some evaluation of Source E (although Source B has been evaluated in the previous paragraph). The use of Source B in a different context to the previous paragraph is interesting – it is a good idea to try to use your sources in different ways.

My enquiry also found evidence to support the interpretation. Source H shows that in World War 2 many more women were employed in the war effort forming 80 per cent of the additional labour force – usually housewives or those with jobs not related to their wartime jobs. Another important difference is that in World War 1 women volunteered for war work. In World War 2 from 1941 onwards women were conscripted to work in war industries – Alice Hewitson *had* to work. Single women were directed to other areas to work on the land or in a munitions factory. Source H is a secondary source written by an historian 40 years after the war. It can be accepted as reliable.

Women also had some different roles in the two World Wars and in World War 2 they covered more areas. So it could be said that their role was greater in World War 2. Source F shows women being used in World War 1 in a less important role. The men are going off to war and the role of women is to encourage them to do so. This is a recruitment poster issued by the government before conscription was introduced. The poster is exaggerated to get the message over. It cleverly has women (the weaker sex) staying behind to look after the home to persuade men to fight for their protection. It is a piece of propaganda but it is useful in showing how important recruitment was to the British government.

Source G is another government propaganda poster, this time from World War 2. It is different from Source F because it shows women as equals to men in the war effort. The woman in the WAAF is shown to have just as important a role as the RAF pilot – together they will win the war. In World War 1 in 1917 the WAAC was set up to do office jobs in the army. In World War 2 there was the ATS and the WRNS as well as the WAAF. Although many jobs were still backroom, women also worked with men repairing planes and operating radar systems. The poster is useful because it shows how the government in World War 2 now accepted that women had a greater role to play in the war effort. However, it is also propaganda trying to encourage women to join the WAAF. Despite what it shows, women were not equal to men in the RAF. It was the men who did the fighting, women only supported them.

AQA Examiner's comment

This section clearly presents the case for agreeing with the interpretation. Source H is a 'stand alone' although Source B is again brought in. There is some analysis of the source but the knowledge to support it is greater here. The evaluation is rather general. It might have been better to include an additional source from World War 1 to compare with Source H.

Sources F and G are used well to draw a valid contrast between the role of women in the two World Wars. There is good analysis of the meaning of both sources and good evaluation of their reliability and limitations. The knowledge to support the sources is also strong.

I have found evidence to agree and disagree with the interpretation. Sources A, B, C and D show that women had similar roles in both World Wars in two areas that contributed to victory – land and munitions/heavy industry. There is also a similar negative view of women's roles in Sources E and B. On the other hand, Sources F and G show that there were differences in the roles of women and that in World War 2 women played a more active part. Source H shows more women were involved in the war effort in World War 2 than in World War 1. It also adds that women were conscripted in World War 2, something that didn't happen in World War 1.

In World War 1 women's contribution was great considering the status of women at that time. By World War 2 their status was higher and the war was different. It was more all-emcompassing, so women had to do more. So I would say that women *probably* did play a greater part in World War 2 but it was not a *far* greater role.

AQA Examiner's comment

This is a strong conclusion. It is linked directly to the question and to the sources that have been chosen. A judgement is made – it is not one way or the other but sees the merits of both sides of the argument. The use of knowledge in the last paragraph adds to this. The final sentence is a very good summing up of the answer.

▇ Examiner's assessment of the answer

The word count for the answer is about 1,300 words – more than advised in the Specification but there would be no penalty for exceeding the advice.

The strengths of the answer should be obvious. It clearly reaches Level 3:

■ there is good analysis of all sources with the possible exception of Sources G and H

■ there is also good evaluation of all sources, again with the possible exception of Source H

■ the knowledge to support the sources and to point out their limitations is also good.

Now look at the Level 4 mark scheme. In addition to Level 3:

■ the evaluation of the sources is done in depth. Provenance, reliability, utility and limitations are all covered

■ there is a balanced judgement on the evidence of the sources. This is made throughout the answer and is very well summarised in the last paragraph. The candidate shows that the question has been fully understood.

So the answer is in Level 4. The mark range for this level is 21 to 25 marks. The answer should be placed in the middle of the range – 23 is an appropriate mark.

Glossary

A

ARP warden: Air-Raid Precaution warden.

Artefacts: objects from the past that have been found or kept.

B

Battle of Britain: the battle for control of the skies above Britain between the RAF and the *Luftwaffe*, July to September 1940.

C

Component: a discrete assessable element within a controlled assessment/qualification that is not itself formally reported, where the marks are recorded by the awarding body. A component/unit may contain one or more tasks.

Controlled assessment: a form of internal assessment where the control levels are set for each stage of the assessment process: task setting; task taking; and task marking.

Controlled conditions: under examination conditions.

D

Depression: a downturn in the economy of a country. Its common features are a fall in trade, the closure of factories and businesses, and high levels of unemployment. A cycle of depression is formed so that these features keep repeating themselves.

Dole: the popular name for the benefit claimed from the state by the unemployed. All workers contribute to National Insurance while in work and the unemployment benefit comes from this fund.

E

External assessment: a form of independent assessment in which question papers, assignments and tasks are set by awarding body, taken under specified conditions (including detailed supervision and duration) and marked by the awarding body.

G

Glass ceiling: an invisible upper limit. This term was used to describe the limited advancement of women in the workplace due to discrimination, as if there were an invisible ceiling which women could not pass through and so would not be able to rise to the top of the company.

L

Liberal reforms: introduced by the government of the Liberal Party before the First World War. The most important social reforms were Old Age Pensions (1908) and National Insurance (1911).

M

Mark scheme: a scheme detailing how credit is to be awarded in relation to a particular unit, component or task. A mark scheme normally characterises acceptable answers or levels of response to questions/tasks or parts of questions/tasks and identifies the amount of credit each attracts.

Means test: a system introduced by the government to make sure that the unemployment benefit paid out was fair. A person's and a family's sources of income were taken into account in deciding how much benefit a person should receive.

N

National Health Service: a state-operated health service providing free treatment to all people of the country. It is funded by national insurance contributions and taxes.

Nationalisation: the ownership of an industry by the state. Boards like the National Coal Board were set up by the government to run an industry on behalf of the state. There are no private owners in a nationalised industry.

Nationalism: the desire of people of the same nation or country to rule and govern themselves – to gain their independence. A nationalist movement usually seeks to remove an existing government from its control over them.

Nazi–Soviet Pact: the agreement made in August 1939 between Germany and the USSR not to attack each other and to divide Poland between them.

O

Oral source: spoken evidence of an event. It could be a one-to-one interview with a person who has lived through an event, or a recording (on tape or in writing) of a person speaking about an event.

P

Phoney War: the period in autumn 1939 and spring 1940 when Britain was at war with Germany, but there was no actual fighting.

Primary source: produced *at the time* of an event. A newspaper is an obvious example but it could be a diary, a cartoon, a photograph. Primary sources are usually intended for the audience at the time of the event – this makes them useful to historians.

Propaganda: beliefs or information that is spread, often by organisations, in a deliberate way to get a particular response.

S

Secondary source: produced *after* the event. A book written by an historian is an obvious example. This will usually be more balanced and unbiased than a primary source because it has the benefit of hindsight.

Suffrage: the right to vote in public elections.

Suffragists and Suffragettes: Suffragists were generally women who believed that the fight for the right to vote should use only peaceful methods, whereas Suffragettes generally believed in a less law-abiding and even a law-breaking approach to gain voting rights for women.

T

Task: a discrete element of external or controlled assessment that may include examinations, assignments, practical activities and projects.

Task marking: this specifies the way in which credit is awarded for candidates' outcomes. Marking involves the use of mark schemes and/or marking criteria produced by the awarding body.

Task setting: the specification of the assessment requirements. Tasks may be set by awarding bodies and/or teachers, as defined by subject-specific rules. Teacher-set tasks must be developed in line with awarding body specified requirements.

Task taking: the conditions for candidate support and supervision, and the authentication of candidates' work. Task taking may involve different parameters from those used in traditional written examinations, for example, candidates may be allowed supervised access to sources such as the internet.

Triple Alliance: an agreement made by the three biggest trade unions to support one another if one of them was engaged in an industrial dispute. It had been formed before the First World War and was renewed in 1920.

U

U-boat: German: *U-Boot*, or (in full) *Unterseeboot*. English: U-boat or submarine.

Unit: the smallest part of a qualification which is formally reported and can be separately certificated. A unit may comprise separately assessed components.

V

VE Day: 8 May 1945, the day of victory in Europe for the Allies in World War II.

Visual source: includes photographs, paintings, posters, cartoons. These are usually primary sources produced at the time of the event. A film is a visual source that can be primary or secondary, depending on when it is made.

W

Wall Street Crash: in 1929, the value of shares at the New York Stock Exchange on Wall Street plummeted. It caused the collapse of the world's most powerful economy and impacted on other countries' economies worldwide.

WSPU: Women's Social and Political Union.

Index

Acknowledgements

The authors and publisher would like to thank the following for permission to reproduce material:

p8 **B** From *Daily Herald*, 1 January 1947; **C** From *Daily Sketch*, 19 November 1910; p9 D *Haig*, Duff Cooper, 1935-36; **E** *Carrie's War*, Nina Bawden, 1973; p29 C Short extract from LDV Delay Explained, *Daily Telegraph*, 19 June, 1940. Reprinted with permission; p31 E Taken from *Home Front in Britain, 1939-45*, A. and A. Pike, 1985; **F** Margaret Watling, taken from *Evacuees*, M. Brown, 2000; p32 **G** Many Londoners took shelter in underground stations, *News Chronicle*, 16th September, 1940. Reprinted with permission of Solo Syndications; p39 **D** Geoffrey Malins, quoted in *Britain and the Great War*, G. Hetherton, 1998; p42 **J** Quoted in *The Twentieth Century World*, N. DeMarco and R. Radway, from a quote in *The Somme*, L. MacDonald, 1993; p46 **P** Short extract from old *Daily Mail* Article, 1 June, 1940. Reprinted with permission of Solo Syndications; p49 **A** Quoted in *History of the Twentieth Century*, Purnell, 1971; **B** Quoted in *History of the Twentieth Century*, Purnell, 1971; p66 **L** Excerpt from *The English Journey* by J. B. Priestley (© J. B. Priestley) reproduced by permission of PFD; p67 **N** Short extract from *BRITAIN AND EUROPE 1848-1980* by M. Roberts, Longman, 1987. Reprinted with permission of Pearson Education Ltd; p69 **Q** Short extract from *THE ROAD TO WIGAN PIER* by George Orwell (Copyright © George Orwell 1937) reprinted by permission of Bill Hamilton as the Literary Executor of the Estate of the Late Sonia Brownell Orwell and Secker & Warburg Ltd; **R** Taken from *Britain in the 20th Century World*, J. Traynor and E. Wilmot, 1994; p70 **A** Short extract from *NOW THE WAR IS OVER* by Paul Addison, published by Jonathan Cape. Reprinted with permission of David Higham Associates Ltd; **B** Short extract from *'Bevan's fight with the BMA'* by Peter Jenkins. Copyright © Peter Jenkins 1963 is reproduced by permission of PFD (www.pfd.co.uk) on behalf of the Estate of Peter Jenkins; p73 **E** Ministry of Education pamphlet No. 12, 1947; p80 **C** Short extract from sound archive IWM ref 511/8/5 Alice Cristobel Remington, Imperial War Museum. Reprinted with permission; **D** From a letter written to the *Liverpool Echo*, 1911; p85 **L** Short extract from *TEMPESTUOUS JOURNEY: Lloyd George His Life and Times* by Frank Owen, published by Hutchinson. Reprinted by permission of The Random House Group Limited; p86 **N** Short extract adapted from *Punch Magazine*, June, 1916. Reprinted with permission of Punch Limited; p 99 **C** Short extract adapted from *'Hindsight'* Volume 18, No 3, September, 2002 by Nick Poyntz. Reprinted with permission of Philip Allan Updates; p103 **D** Mrs Grace Elsey from *WAR WOMEN OF BRITAIN* produced by Imperial War Museum. Reprinted with permission; **E** Short extract from *WAR AND SOCIETY IN BRITAIN 1899-1948* by Rex Pope published by Longman, 1991. Reprinted with permission; **H** Short extract from *BRITISH SOCIETY 1914-1945* by John Stevenson (Penguin Books 1984) Copyright © John Stevenson, 1984. Reprinted with permission of Penguin Books UK

Photographs courtesy of:

© **Abram Games Estate** p36 left; **Advertising Archive** p26; **Anne Ronan Picture Library** pp24 top, 34 bottom left, 52, 54, 64, 68 left, 87 top, 87 centre, 87 bottom, 99; **Corbis**: p56; Corbis/© Robbie Jack p39; © Bettmann/CORBIS pp18 banner, 60 banner, 98 banner; © Underwood & Underwood/CORBIS p78 banner; **Edimedia Archive** p43 top; **getty images** pp18, 30, 62, 65, 67, 68 right, 72, 95 top; **John Frost Newspaper Archive** pp63 bottom, 98 bottom; **2007 Eamonn McCormack** p96; **Photo12** pp32 left, 55; **Popperfoto/Getty Images** p38 banner; **Sante Collection** p41; © **Jack Sullivan / Alamy** p6; **topfoto** pp10, 12, 25, 27, 29, 32 right, 33 left, 33 right, 34 bottom right, 35 right, 36 right, 43 bottom, 44, 45, 63 top, 75, 80, 81, 84, 89, 90 left, 90 right, 91 top, 91 bottom, 93, 95 bottom, 98 top, 102, 103 top, 103 bottom; **World History Archive** pp11, 13, 19, 20 left, 20 right, 21, 24 bottom, 33 centre, 34 top, 35 left, 38 bottom, 40, 47, 60, 82, 103 centre

Front cover photograph © Mary Evans Picture Library / Alamy